SEEKING THE TRUTH OF
CHANGE IN THE CHURCH

SEEKING THE TRUTH OF CHANGE IN THE CHURCH

Reception, Communion and the
Ordination of Women

Edited by
Paul Avis

T & T CLARK INTERNATIONAL
A Continuum imprint
LONDON • NEW YORK

T&T CLARK LTD
A Continuum imprint

The Tower Building
11 York Road
London SE1 7NX, UK

15 East 26th Street
New York, NY 10010
USA

www.continuumbooks.com

Copyright © T&T Clark Ltd, 2004

Considerable efforts have been made to contact copyright holders. In the few cases where this has not been successful, copyright holder should contact T&T Clark at Continuum to resolve the permission.

British Library Cataloguing-in-Publication Data
A catalogue record for this book is available from the British Library

ISBN 0 567 08901 0 (Hardback)
ISBN 0 567 08884 7 (Paperback)

Typeset by YHT Ltd, London
Printed and bound in Great Britain by Cromwell Press, Trowbridge

CONTENTS

LIST OF CONTRIBUTORS

Paul Avis is General Secretary of the Council for Christian Unity of the Church of England, Director of the Centre for the Study of the Christian Church and Sub-Dean of Exeter.

Robert Hannaford is Professor of Theology at St Martin's College, Lancaster, and an Honorary Canon of Chichester.

Christopher Hill is Bishop of Stafford in the Diocese of Lichfield.

John Hind is Bishop of Chichester and Chairman of the Church of England's Faith and Order Advisory Group.

Paul Richardson is Assistant Bishop in the Diocese of Newcastle.

Geoffrey Rowell is Bishop of Gibraltar in Europe.

William G. Rusch is Executive Director: Foundation for a Conference on Faith and Order in North America.

Mary Tanner was formerly Moderator of the World Council of Churches' Faith and Order Commission and General Secretary of the Church of England's Council for Christian Unity.

EDITOR'S PREFACE

The ordination of women as priests in the Church of England continues to generate controversy more than a decade after the decision of the General Synod that made it possible. While the priestly ministry of women has been welcomed in the vast majority of parishes of the Church of England, where it raises hardly a ripple of dissent, the arguments about its merits have not gone away. This book grapples with some of those arguments.

The main focus is on two connected issues. The first is the question of what is meant by 'reception' (the process of discerning the truth of a development in the life of the Church). The second concerns the practice of 'communion' (the unique quality of interpersonal relationships in the Church, that we enter into through baptism, faith and the gift of the Holy Spirit). Perhaps the sharpest challenge posed by this book is: Can we expect to be guided by the Spirit in the process of reception unless we are in communion with those with whom we profoundly disagree?

Several questions that still need answering cluster around the ordination of women in the Church of England (and in the Anglican Communion more widely). There is the question about the authority of one church to take a decision in a matter that affects the whole Church. There is the question of the ecumenical consequences of this action, its effect on relations with the Roman Catholic Church and the Eastern churches (though of course the ecumenical argument cuts the other way with Lutheran, Reformed, Methodist and Baptist churches). And there are several questions about the arrangements that the Church of England put in place to enable those opposed in conscience to the decision to remain within the Church of England.

Many people in the churches have heard of 'flying bishops' and may know that they are related to something called 'the Act of Synod'. The Episcopal Ministry Act of Synod 1993 makes provision for extended (not alternative) episcopal ministry (pastoral and sacramental) for clergy and parishes that request it in a diocese where the bishop has ordained women priests. This pastoral care is offered at the invitation of the diocesan bishop, whose formal oversight as the 'chief pastor' of the diocese is protected. This provision is a lifeline to some, enabling them to stay within the Church of England, but a source of puzzlement and even outrage to others because it seems to discriminate against women priests.

The Act of Synod is made to take the blame for the impairment of communion within the Church of England. What is not always realized is that 'no-go areas' for women priests were provided for in the 1992 legislation to permit the ordination of women (in the form of Resolutions A and B). It is only extended episcopal care that is the subject of the 1993 Act of Synod. The Provincial Episcopal Visitors (the so-called flying bishops) are simply one of three possible ways of providing this care – the other two being diocesan and regional arrangements among the bishops more locally.

The Act of Synod has been dubbed an 'act of folly' in a volume of essays edited by Monica Furlong and published by SCM Press in 1998 (*Act of Synod: Act of Folly*). It is easy to pillory it as that title does (though the book contains some searching questions, especially those posed by the Revd Canon Dr Judith Maltby, to the rationale of the Act). There is now a ginger group dedicated to the repeal of the 1993 Act of Synod.

The contributors to the present volume are divided – pretty evenly, I think – over the issue of the ordination of women. But they are united in supporting the 1993 Act of Synod. They all believe that it is defensible; that it is

probably necessary; and that – when it is properly understood – it makes better ecclesiological sense than it is often
credited with.

The essays in this book emerged from two consultations
that I convened, under the auspices of the Centre for the
Study of the Christian Church, at St George's House,
Windsor Castle, with Canon Laurence Gunner in 1998 and
2000 respectively. The Centre is based at Exeter Cathedral
and the University of Exeter and promotes the scholarly
study of the Christian Church – especially its mission,
ministry and unity. The Centre is involved in the *International Journal for the Study of the Christian Church*, published
by T&T Clark/Continuum.

These chapters are offered as a contribution to mutual
understanding among all Christians, the strengthening of
communion among Anglicans, and a clearer grasp of what
reception and communion mean in an ecumenical context.

PAUL AVIS

THE LANDSCAPE OF RECEPTION

William G. Rusch

The subject of this essay is ecumenical reception. A convenient way to address the topic is to imagine a map of the landscape of reception. Such a map would be no simple representation, for the landscape of reception has become not only more cluttered but confused in recent years. It is tempting to declare that the map reads, *terra incognita*, or perhaps in medieval terms, 'Here be dragons!' But such an exclamation would not do justice to our topic.

Actually the cartography of reception is vast – to use this helpful image – and we must first narrow our focus and then increase the scale if we are to have some clarity about this subject.

Reception as a concept is multidimensional. It has a referent in the area of legal scholarship, where it refers to the transfer of Roman law at the end of the Middle Ages into European, and especially German, law. Scholarly attention to this phenomenon began in the seventeenth century and continued through the twentieth century.[1]

Reception has appeared in the study of literature in the last half of the last century with concepts of 'Wirkungsgeschichte' and 'Rezeptionsgeschichte', where the inter-

---

[1] Franz Wieacker, *Privatrechtsgeschichte der Neuzeit unter besonderer Berücksichtigung der deutschen Entwicklung*, 2nd edn (Göttingen: Vandenhoeck & Ruprecht, 1967).

relationship of the reader to the text is explored.[2] In philosophy, reception has been employed to describe an intellectual and cultural change, notably in the work of Hans-Georg Gadamer, but there are other examples.[3]

These legal, literary and philosophical areas of the map may be folded aside, with the notation that there are some rich veins to be explored there for an understanding of reception, but that there is not the leisure for that investigation at this time. In fact, a new insight is that these areas of reception can add much to our primary area of attention as the thesis of Ormond Rush on *The Reception of Doctrine* reveals.[4]

However, concentration must be given to that part of the chart where reception as an ecclesiological process is indicated. It is often stated that reception precedes the Church itself.[5] This is certainly true in the sense that the Church arose out of the continuing process of reception. In the Old Testament it is possible to discern the motifs of receiving and re-receiving. Creation receives its being from God. Human beings receive God's revelation; Israel received the covenant.

The New Testament makes clear that Christ receives his mission from the Father. The Church as the community of faith receives from Christ. Paul reminds the Corinthians that they have received the gospel. Despite differences of detail, the various books of the New Testament describe a process of reception that is not legal and formal but a glad

---

[2] E.g. Edgar V. McKnight, *The Bible and the Reader: An Introduction to Literary Criticism* (Philadelphia: Fortress Press, 1985) and Bernard C. Lategan and William S. Vorster, *Text and Reality: Aspects of Reference in Biblical Texts* (Philadelphia: Fortress Press, 1985).

[3] Hans-Georg Gadamer, *Truth and Method* (New York: Continuum, 1975).

[4] Ormond Rush, *The Reception of Doctrine: An Appropriation of Hans Robert Jauss' Reception Aesthetics and Literary Hermeneutics* (Rome: Editrice Pontificia Università Gregoriana, 1997).

[5] E.g. John Zizioulas, 'The Theological Problem of Reception', *Centro pro Unione Bulletin* 26 (1984): 3.

process of receiving the good news of the gospel and the Lord himself. This is always an event of the Holy Spirit. In the biblical sense, reception is one of the main characteristics of the Christian faith itself. Thus reception is an invaluable biblical concept, often present without the specific words of *lambanein* or *dechesthai*, or the Latin terms, *receptio* and *recipere*.

In the pre-Constantinian period reception was primarily concerned with the process by which local and regional synods were made known and accepted by other local churches. The Early Church saw itself as a fellowship of churches involved in the process of giving and taking from one another. In all these instances what is seen is a beginning of a spiritual process of reception by the entire community rather than a juridical action. A new factor appears in the Constantinian and post-Constantinian eras when the emperor becomes directly involved, and council decisions acquire the status of imperial law. Yet even here reception is a process where laity, monks and church leaders participate with an enthusiasm that would seem strange to many today. This reception was determined by two principal ideas: *consensio antiquitatis* and *consensio universitatis*.[6] Without both forms of consensus, the decisions of any council had little chance of reception.

Of course, reception in the Early Church was taking place in areas besides that of the decisions of councils. In the areas of liturgy, local laws and customs, and the canon of Scripture itself, a process of reception was moving forward. Implicit in the practice was the view of the Church as a community of local churches in fellowship, *communio*, with each other, having gifts to share and a faith to be handed down from generation to generation.

Some of these factors, notably an ecclesiology of local

---

[6] Hermann Josef Sieben, *Die Konzilidee der Alten Kirche*, Konzilen-Geschichte series B, Untersuchungen (Paderborn: Schöningh, 1979), pp. 511–16.

churches, did not continue in the West in the Middle Ages. The sixteenth-century Reformation was in part a reaction against the ever-increasing papal domination of the Church. The Reformation itself caused the reception, or non-reception, of new documents such as the Lutheran Confessions and the decisions of the Council of Trent, 1545–63.[7] This general description of reception is as true for the Eastern churches as it is for the Church in the West, although Orthodoxy considered reception in the light of a total ecclesiology, and not limited to statements of the magisterium in legal categories. For the East, reception involves agreement with the faith of the Church as the final authority. It is the fruit of the charismatic work of the Spirit. The Orthodox churches see in reception a dialectic between the laity and the clergy, both of whom have a critical role under the inspiration of the Spirit.[8]

The ecclesiastical process outlined here, a process before the rise of the modern ecumenical movement, has been described as *classical reception*. It shares several characteristics. This classical reception was never merely the acceptance of theological texts from church councils. It was never merely a juridical process. Rather, reception always functioned as a continuing, ongoing process that in a sense predated the institution of the Church. It includes the receipt of God's love in his Son as well as the acceptance of a history and a tradition. It involves the constant practice of interpretation and reinterpretation. This reception is not repristination, but it is a lively process of the Church drawing from the resources of the past to seize and accept the present activities of its loving Lord.[9]

This part of the map is fascinating and in some ways

---

[7] For a general historical survey see William G. Rusch, *Reception: An Ecumenical Opportunity* (Philadelphia: Fortress Press, 1988), pp. 31–48.

[8] Waclaw Hryniewicz, 'Die ekklesiale Rezeption in der Sicht der orthodoxen Theologie', *Theologie und Glaube* 65 (1975): 260–63.

[9] Rusch, *Reception*, p. 53.

directly relevant for the journey, but it is not the proper goal of the travel. In fact, for many years this section of the terrain was seriously neglected. In 1977 Franz Wolfinger in an important article wondered whether reception had been forgotten in the Church. This estimate was correct, for apart from the reflections of some patristic and medieval scholars interested in church councils, discussions of reception had almost disappeared from theological literature before 1959.[10]

It was Pope John XXIII's dramatic calling of the Second Vatican Council that raised questions for the ecumenical movement and the Roman Catholic Church about the conciliar nature of the Church, teaching authority, and how conciliar decisions were *received* in the Church. The Second Vatican Council moved reception to the centre of attention. It became a topic of intense ecumenical interest. This early renewal of interest was largely characterized by concern with *conciliar* reception. It looked back to the Early Church and to the Orthodox churches as resources. Yet this interest had more than a historical motivation. There was an eagerness to see how reception could become a resource for enabling divided churches to move closer to unity. Another factor was the Roman Catholic Church's own reception of its own council. How would Catholicism receive the Second Vatican Council?[11] Quickly a considerable body of literature developed in Roman Catholic and ecumenical circles.[12]

There is one more reason for the contemporary interest in reception, and in fact in many ways it has become more significant than the Second Vatican Council, although it is

---

[10] Franz Wolfinger, 'Die Rezeption theologischer Einsichten und ihre theologische und ökumenische Bedeutung: Von der Einsicht zur Verwirklichung', *Catholica* 31 (1977): 202–33.

[11] Jean-Marie Tillard, 'Did We Receive Vatican II?', *One in Christ* 4 (1985): 276–83.

[12] See Gilles Routhier, *La Réception d'un concile* (Paris: Editions du Cerf, 1993), pp. 246–55.

directly related to it. The council authorized the entrance of the Roman Catholic Church into the one ecumenical movement. This approval has resulted in a proliferation of ecumenical dialogues or bilateral conversations. These conversations undertaken by officially appointed representatives of two churches, two traditions, or two confessional families, with purposes ranging from promoting mutual understanding to achieving full communion, or full visible unity, have increased dramatically in the last 37 or so years. The literature on these regional and international dialogues and their reports is well known and extensive, as the new edition of *Growth in Agreement* now illustrates.[13]

Certainly beginning in the mid to late 1970s, and throughout the 1980s and 1990s, the dialogues were pressing their sponsoring churches to enter into a process of reception of their work and to move forward toward full communion. A new kind of reception was being envisioned, *ecumenical reception.* Thus in 1983 Thomas Ryan, just six years after Wolfinger, described 'reception' as the new 'holy word' of the ecumenical movement.[14] Obviously something had happened between 1977 and 1983. The process has continued to accelerate into the twenty-first century. That something was 'bilateral ecumenical dialogue'.

When in 1988 I wrote my book *Reception: An Ecumenical Opportunity*, reflection on ecumenical reception was in an early stage. I stated my purpose was to review the discussion of ecumenical reception in the periodical literature and to

---

[13] Harding Meyer and Lukas Vischer (eds), *Growth in Agreement: Reports and Agreements of Ecumenical Conversations on a World Level* (New York and Ramsey, NJ: Paulist Press, 1984), and Jeffrey Gros, FSC, Harding Meyer and William G. Rusch (eds), *Growth in Agreement II: Reports and Agreed Statements of Ecumenical Conversations on a World Level, 1982–1998* (Geneva: World Council Publications; Grand Rapids, MI: Eerdmans, 2000).

[14] Thomas Ryan, 'Reception: Unpacking the New Holy Word', *Ecumenism* 82 (1983): 27–34.

offer a number of suggestions for the future. There were very few full-length treatments of ecumenical reception or encyclopedia articles. I said that I saw my volume as standing between the constantly growing body of articles on the topic and the major treatise to be written eventually.[15]

Deliberation was beginning, but there were very few concrete examples of churches *receiving* the work of their dialogues. Since then, the situation has changed conspicuously. Gilles Routhier in his *La Réception d'un concile* has given us a bibliography of more than nineteen pages, and this is a list drawn up several years ago![16] Not only was literature on the subject growing, but examples of reception have begun to emerge, or at least examples of initial stages of reception, globally and nationally. To return to the image of the map, where earlier editions might have shown a small village with the name of 'ecumenical reception' by the turn of this century in terms of literary and ecumenical attention with specific results, the map would have to indicate an ever-growing urban sprawl. It is here on the map that the journey should end, and the scale of the map should be increased to examine more closely ecumenical reception.

Already some years ago, the Dominican theologian Jean Marie Tillard offered some sound advice for discussing ecumenical reception. He pointed out that reviving the word 'reception' after so much neglect carried a certain danger. If used without adequate concern, the word may become an umbrella term, a catch-all. If 'reception' means everything, it will finally mean nothing.[17] There is already evidence that reception is viewed as reconciliation of a

---

[15] See note 7, above.
[16] See note 12, above.
[17] Jean-Marie Tillard, '"Reception": A Time to Beware of False Steps', *Ecumenical Trends* 14 (1985): 145–8.

superficial sort.[18] The potential that the reception process holds for the ecumenical present and future will be lost if reception is understood as simply the re-establishment of cordial relations.

Ecumenical reception must be perceived as foremost a spiritual process. This does not make ecumenical reception vague or abstract. Rather, it protects it from being viewed as only a sociological process or a democratic movement looking for a majority vote. The awareness that reception operates under the Spirit keeps the churches open to a common fidelity to the mind and will of Christ himself.

From these comments, it becomes apparent how critical a definition of this concept of ecumenical reception is. Back in 1988 I noted how initial and partial the experience of ecumenical reception was. Nevertheless, I offered a preliminary definition, which I would suggest is still valid. I wrote that ecumenical reception includes

> all phases and aspects of an ongoing process by which a church under the guidance of God's Spirit makes the results of a bilateral or a multilateral conversation a part of its faith and life because the results are seen to be in conformity with the teachings of Christ and of the apostolic community, that is, the gospel as witnessed to in Scripture.[19]

I believe that this definition is in harmony with the views of Yves Congar, who in 1972 in an acclaimed article wrote:

> By reception we mean the process by which a church tradition appropriates a truth which has not arisen out of that tradition, but which it yet recognizes and adopts as a formulation of the faith. In the process of reception we understand something other

[18] For example, see two recent instances of the Evangelical Lutheran Church in America, where in one case a bilateral ecumenical agreement was amended unilaterally by this church, which causes serious problems of an understanding of full communion, and where in another case this church formed an association with the Consultation on Church Union without exploring the confessional and ecumenical implications of such an action.

[19] Rusch, *Reception*, p. 31.

than what the Scholastics meant by obedience. For them, this was the act whereby a subordinate regulated his will and his conduct according to the legitimate precepts of a superior, out of respect for his/her authority. Reception is not merely the expression of the relationship *secundum et supra*; it includes the active giving of assent, even the exercise of judgement, where the life of a body which draws upon its original spiritual resources is expressed.[20]

There are obviously differences between classical reception and ecumenical reception, although there are also similarities. Classical reception is mainly associated with the councils of the Church, and in a period before the rise of the modern ecumenical movement. It included the acceptance of liturgies, prayers and formulations of doctrine, which were viewed as enriching the entire Church – a Church seen, for all its variation, as a united Church, where the bishop and the local community played key roles.

The context of ecumenical reception is not one united Church. Instead there are divided churches that are called to receive from one another. In this setting what is sought is not simply agreement in doctrine, but mutual ecclesial reception. This raises questions about the continuity of individual churches with the past, about the identification of appropriate organs within these bodies for reception, and about how reception is possible within an incomplete or broken eucharistic community. For the first time churches are being asked in ecumenical reception to receive materials they did not directly produce. This reception involves a fundamental sharing in the one apostolic faith as it has been handed down in many communities of faith. The Church communities since the early 1970s have been struggling to reinterpret their common heritage with new language, new

---

[20] Y. Congar, 'La "Réception" comme réalité ecclésiologique', *Revue des sciences philosophiques et théologiques* 56 (1972): 369–403. English transl.: 'Reception as an Ecclesiological Reality', in *Election and Consensus in the Church*, ed. G. Alberigo and A. Weiler, *Concilium* 77 (New York: Herder & Herder, 1972): 45.

emphases, and new insights – all acquired by participation in the one ecumenical movement. It is easy to see why reception of this nature has represented a major challenge to the churches. We should not have been surprised to learn how difficult and arduous it was going to be. Exactly 20 years ago now at Lima, speaking of *Baptism, Eucharist and Ministry*, Dom Emmanuel Lanne stated, 'It is also essential that all the churches see their reception of this document concerns them at the very center of their being. What is at stake here is the full communion which they desire to recover and the visible unity to which they are called.'[21]

It is helpful to see ecumenical reception as a comprehensive approach and not only the receiving of ecumenical documents. The final aim of ecumenical reception is not to receive or to ratify documents, but rather to realize and manifest visible unity between the churches. In a profound sense, this reception begins with the establishment of a dialogue and continues on after the dialogue reports and its work is accepted by the churches. Günther Gassmann has helped us when he suggested that ecumenical reception should seek to receive the *dialogue event as a whole*.[22] Thus we are reminded that the official response by church leaders to the text, and the use of the text in various ways within each church, is only part of a broader reception process.

André Birmelé stresses, perhaps more than I would be willing to do, the similarities between classical and ecumenical reception, although I certainly do not deny them.[23]

---

[21] Emmanuel Lanne, 'The Problem of "Reception" ', in Michael Kinnamon (ed.), *Towards Visible Unity: Commission on Faith and Order Lima, 1982*, vol. 1, Faith and Order paper 112 (Geneva: World Council of Churches, 1982), p. 53.

[22] Günther Gassman, 'Rezeption im ökumenischen Kontext', *Ökumenische Rundschau* 33 (1984): 357–68.

[23] André Birmelé. 'La Réception comme exigence oecuménique', in G.R. Evans and M. Gourgues (eds), *Communion et réunion: Mélanges J.-M.R. Tillard* (Leuven: Leuven University Press, 1995), pp. 75–94.

But he is exceptionally helpful in reminding us of the differences and specific difficulties of ecumenical reception. For example, Birmelé points out there is an unusual character to ecumenical reception. It requires a creativity and the presence of structures and instruments which most churches did not previously possess. Ecumenical reception must take place locally, but local ecumenism has often been left out of the dialogue process. Related to this point is the fact that dialogue texts are the work of specialists, worked out dialogically, but now they must be received monologically or mono-confessionally. Ecumenical reception has been hindered by the lack of a final answer to the questions of models of unity. What should our desired unity look like? Also, ecumenical reception has suffered from difficulties about the extent and content of consensus required for reception. To illustrate this point, let mention be made of ministry! Finally Birmelé mentions the issue of authority. Where and what is the authority in each of our churches to receive dialogue results in a binding manner?

In view of such obstacles, it is remarkable that ecumenical reception has occurred at all, but it has, and in most instances since I wrote my book on reception. I want to examine briefly a few examples and then draw some conclusions why ecumenical reception was possible. The examination could be done by chapter and verse in some detail, but there is not space for this exercise. The choice is also arbitrary, with the exception that the Anglican–Roman Catholic International Commission is excluded because in these circles it is so well known. Yet I believe this process will carry the discussion beyond that of ten or twelve years ago and give us some new insights about the requirement for this type of reception between churches and perhaps within a church. The latter point is especially relevant to debates raging within individual churches.

The first document to be noted here is *The Porvoo Common Statement* of 1993 between Anglicans and Lutherans in

Europe.[24] Even a cursory glance at this text discloses several critical points. The first section stresses the commonality of the churches in faith and in mission. The second portion describes the nature and unity of the Church, highlighting both the newness of the present situation and the common understanding of the Church shared by Anglicans and Lutherans; but this joint comprehension also acknowledges a diversity. This diversity is affirmed in its richness and not merely noted in a begrudging manner. The next block of text delineates an agreement in faith. But it is extremely important to observe this agreement is nuanced in the text. It is substantial; there is a high degree of consensus. Then it is declared there is a high degree of unity in faith and doctrine. In the fourth section on episcopacy and apostolicity, there is recognition both of a convergence on these topics and a difference in that churches have been faithful to their apostolic calling by more than one means of continuity.

In summary, *The Porvoo Common Statement* indicates, or strongly suggests, that there is a far-reaching, not total, agreement between Anglicans and Lutherans on faith, mission and ministry, and this allows a new stage on the journey together in faith without a denial by Anglicans or Lutherans of a particularity within their own churches, i.e. views of historic episcopal succession.

The second dialogue report to be examined is *Following Our Shepherd to Full Communion*, the report of the Lutheran–Moravian dialogue in the United States.[25] Here Lutherans and Moravians speak of their different yet complementary theologies. This theme is repeated in the text. The document indicates Lutheran and Moravian theological methods

---

[24] *Together in Mission and Ministry: The Porvoo Common Statement with Essays on Church and Ministry in Northern Europe* (London: Church House Publishing, 1993).

[25] *Following Our Shepherd to Full Communion: Report of the Lutheran–Moravian Dialogue with Recommendations for Full Communion in Worship, Fellowship and Mission* (Chicago: Evangelical Lutheran Church in America, 1998).

differ from each other, and yet the differences are mutually supportive. In major sections the text speaks of mutual affirmations and complementarities. These mutual complementarities disclose diversity within the context of unity. Yet the nature of diversity is seen as completing and enhancing.

Thus *Following Our Shepherd to Full Communion* argues that Lutherans and Moravians share a convergence of faith that is less than total and allows for significant diversity between them. Still on this basis, Lutherans and Moravians in the United States were able to make the juridical decision to move into a relation of full communion in which each keeps its particular identity, and in fact is not asked to surrender but affirm it.

The third example is the *Leuenberg Agreement* of 1973, originally involving Lutherans and Reformed in Europe, but subsequently signed by a number of churches throughout the world.[26] This document brings the churches that sign it into a relation of church fellowship or full communion. This is possible according to the *Leuenberg Agreement* because a necessary and sufficient, but not total, consensus exists on a number of topics which in the past were deemed church-dividing, e.g. baptism, the Lord's Supper, Christology and predestination. It is a consensus about central matters. Thus, the condemnations of the Reformation confessions are inapplicable today. The limits of the consensus are shown in the call for further study of the differences in doctrine which still continue in the participating churches. Still the *Leuenberg Agreement* is clear that it is consensus that is the basis for church fellowship among the churches. In this agreement the churches do not lose their confessional identity.

---

[26] James E. Andrews and Joseph A. Burgess (eds), *An Invitation to Action: The Lutheran–Reformed Dialogue, Series III, 1981–83* (Philadelphia: Fortress Press, 1984), pp. 61–73.

The last instance here is the *Formula of Agreement* between the Evangelical Lutheran Church in America and three churches of the Reformed tradition in the United States.[27] This document, whose juridical acceptance is the basis for full communion between/among these four churches, declares there is a doctrinal consensus shared by these churches. This consensus is grounded in the New Testament and evidenced in the core traditions within the one, holy, catholic and apostolic Church. The consensus is in the common core. At the same time there are differences which can be understood today, if they were not in the sixteenth century, as diverse witnesses to the one gospel. This diversity within a common confession gives a complementarity. The remaining differences are acknowledged even to the extent of their irreconcilability. What is determinative is the inherent unity in Christ, so that the remaining differences are not viewed as Church-dividing. In this context of core consensus and remaining difference the *Formula of Agreement* describes a hermeneutic of 'mutual affirmation and admonition'. The text offers a major section on the 'fundamental doctrinal consensus' – a consensus in justification, sacraments, ministry, and church and world. Then there is a section on 'differing emphases' taking up the condemnations, the presence of Christ and predestination. This section reveals the continuing differences on these themes. The conclusion of the *Formula of Agreement* is that a fundamental doctrinal consensus exists and is sufficient for a relation of full communion, where confessional identity and differences continue. But the fundamental, not total, consensus with confessional diversity allows for a

---

[27] *A Formula of Agreement between the Evangelical Lutheran Church in America, the Presbyterian Church (USA), the Reformed Church in America and the United Church of Christ on entering into Full Communion on the basis of a Common Calling* (Chicago: Evangelical Lutheran Church in America, 1996).

binding and effective commitment to full communion for these churches.

This succinct analysis could be pursued in a number of ways. For immediate purposes the discussion will be limited to the methodology which is disclosed.[28] What these dialogues show, and others could be mentioned to reveal the same thing, is that the bilateral conversations are rooted clearly in the New Delhi declaration of the World Council of Churches and its commentary from 1961.[29]

Yet the dialogues differ from New Delhi on one specific point, namely the problem of unity and diversity. Now diversity has always been affirmed in the ecumenical movement over against uniformity. But in the early decades of the ecumenical movement the notion was commonplace that confessional diversities had to pass away. Thus, the early promotion of organic union took place in the first Faith and Order conferences.

This situation changed with the entrance of the Roman Catholic Church into the one ecumenical movement in the late 1960s. This church's self-understanding and its disposition toward bilateral dialogue as a favoured form of ecumenism gave confessionality a positive meaning in a way that the multilateral efforts had not. In the dialogues there arose an understanding of church unity that was no longer dominated by a contradiction between confession and ecumenism. 'Unity and reconciled diversity' became the goal of the dialogues, whether or not this precise phrase was employed. Confessional particularity was not lost, but it

---

[28] In the argumentation which follows I am particularly indebted to the insights of Harding Meyer, especially as found in his important article, 'Die Prägung einer Formel: Ursprung und Intention', in Harald Wagner, (ed.), *Einheit–Aber Wie?: Zur Tragfähigkeit der ökumenischen Formel vom 'differenzierten Konsen'*, Quaestiones Disputatae 184 (Freiburg im Bresgau: Herder, 2000), pp. 36–58.

[29] *The New Delhi Report: The Third Assembly of the World Council of Churches, 1961* (London: SCM Press, 1961), pp. 116–19.

was rather affirmed as legitimate. Thus dialogues had to develop an understanding of church unity/*koinonia*, a fellowship of churches of different confessions, which had as its goal not the removal or standardization of confessional diversity but a reconciliation/overcoming of the Church-dividing character. This means that over time and as a result of dialogue work, a specific type of consensus arose. This consensus was not there before the dialogues, but it is a product of the dialogue experience.

What the dialogues have done is *not* to seek in their efforts for understanding and consensus to merge different doctrines into a synthesis, in one common doctrine of a particular subject. Rather the dialogues seek to place differing doctrines in a new common relationship. The consensus defines and describes this new common relationship. Indeed the consensus *is* this new common relationship. It is critical to stress that this approach is not a mere compromise or a pluralism of opinions. It is not a questionable hermeneutical trick!

This consensus, more and more being described as a *differentiated consensus*, is characterized by a consciously intended double structure, by a clear bi-dimensionality.[30] On one level there is a fundamental commonality; on a second level there are remaining differences. Thus there is in the dialogue reports an affirmation of a consensus on basic truths regarding a specific doctrine or issue. In view of this consensus the remaining differences on this doctrine or issue are tolerable, bearable. The different explications by each side of the dialogue in their difference are open to each other and do not destroy the consensus in regard to the basic truths.

It is therefore a consensus, which does not exclude under all circumstances difference as something foreign to it, but it allows room for difference in itself and integrates dif-

---

[30] Meyer, 'Die Prägung einer Formel', pp. 54–5.

ferences. This means that differentiated consensus always comprises two different statements: (1) a statement which expresses in fundamental and essential content the agreement attained on a doctrine or point that until now was disputed and (2) a statement which indicates how and why the remaining differences can be evaluated as admissible and thus do not call into question the agreement in its fundamental and essential aspects.

The conclusion to be drawn from all this is rather direct and simple. Ecumenical reception has been, and will be in the future, possible only on the basis of an effective concept of *differentiated consensus*, a concept which arose in contemporary bilateral conversations with their specific understanding of church unity/*koinonia*, a fellowship of churches of different confessions, as an expressed idea of the goal.

How this insight relates to the internal life of individual churches, which have made unilateral decisions for themselves, but choices that have considerable ecumenical implications, cannot be addressed here. It is obviously a closely related topic.

It would seem that there are only two other alternatives for churches in the ecumenical movement if they reject differentiated consensus. The first is that one church gives up the position held until now and takes over the view of the other church. The second is that both churches somehow free themselves from their previous positions on a specific topic and develop a new position or statement. It is difficult to see how either of these two approaches would ever be attainable.

It is probably time to fold up that map. As we conclude, an image used by Harding Meyer, which is closely related to landscapes and maps, might be helpful.[31] Meyer spoke of

---

[31] Harding Meyer, ' Rezeption–vom Konsens zur Gemeinschaft', in H. Fries (ed.), *Das Ringen um die Einheit der Christen* (Düsseldorf: Patmos, 1983), p. 172.

the work of ecumenical dialogues as the discovery of a new land. He went on to say that reception is the opening and settling of that new land. His conclusion was that the settlement may take more time, patience and effort than the discovery. Perhaps those involved ecumenically are just beginning to grasp how accurate this insight is. Yet the journey and the settling are both not options for the followers of that One, who prayed for the unity of God's people in Christ.

2

RECEPTION
Towards an Anglican Understanding

Paul Avis

'Reception' is a notion that is itself in the process of being 'received'. It is an emerging idea that is still imperfectly understood. The nature of reception is being actively reflected upon and critically assimilated throughout the Christian Church.[1] There is an intriguing reflexivity in the concept of reception. As we apply the notion of reception to particular, concrete issues in the life of the churches, so we clarify the idea itself. And as we become clearer about the idea, so, in turn, it sheds light on developments in Christian theology and practice. An approach to this elusive topic involves a kind of methodological spiral.

Reception is a phenomenon that has always characterized the life of the Church. It is not peculiar to the controversial circumstances surrounding the ordination of women in modern Anglicanism. It is endemic to the living, moving story of church history and applies to the whole scope of unceasing development in theology, worship and mission. But, as an idea, 'reception' is comparatively young and undeveloped. The nature of reception varies from one context to another. It is, therefore, continually being adapted and adjusted to meet fresh demands. Not the least challenging of these new contexts with their fresh demands on the idea of reception is the decision of the Church of

[1] For a general introduction to the concept see W.G. Rusch, *Reception: An Ecumenical Opportunity*, (Philadelphia: Fortress Press/Lutheran World Federation, 1988).

England, within the Anglican Communion, to admit women to the ministerial priesthood, or presbyterate, of the Church.

Two Basic Concepts of Reception

The idea of reception, like the ideas of collegiality and of primacy, derives originally from the ecclesiology of the Roman Catholic Church. In its Roman Catholic context it refers primarily to the process of assimilation and acceptance by the faithful of teachings or decisions of the magisterium. This assimilation is seen as largely passive: acceptance is an act of obedience to those – the college of bishops headed by the Pope, but in practice mainly the Pope himself – who are appointed to teach, rule and guide the Church. This sense is still very much the operative one in Roman Catholic ecclesiology.

For example, a substantial discussion of reception by J.M.R. Tillard concerns the reception in the Roman Catholic Church of the teaching of the Second Vatican Council.[2] Although the idea of reception could never be monolithic or lacking in nuance in the hands of a theologian as subtle as Tillard, the fact remains that, in its setting in the Roman Catholic Church, reception has strong overtones of a hierarchical, top-down approach. In the framework of official Roman Catholic teaching, it is for those endowed with appropriate authority to say what is to be believed and what is to be practised. And it is for those who are called to obey and to follow to receive that direction of their faith and morals. As Vatican II insists: 'In matters of faith and morals, the bishops speak in the name of Christ, and the faithful are to accept their teaching and adhere to it with a religious assent of soul.' Even more so must this submission be made to the teaching of the Pope:

[2] J.M.R. Tillard, 'Did we "Receive" Vatican II?', *One in Christ* 21 (1985): 276–83.

'This religious submission of will and of mind must be shown in a special way to the authentic teaching authority of the Roman Pontiff, even when he is not speaking ex cathedra.' The Pope's supreme authority must be acknowledged with reverence and his judgements sincerely adhered to.[3] As the *Catechism of the Catholic Church* makes clear, filial obedience to the Church's teaching and discipline applies no less in the area of morals than it does in the area of doctrine. The faithful 'have the *duty* of observing the constitutions and decrees conveyed by the legitimate authority of the Church. Even if they concern disciplinary matters, these determinations call for docility in charity.' While acknowledging the role of conscience, the *Catechism* insists that 'Personal conscience and reason should not be set in opposition to the moral law or the Magisterium of the Church.'[4]

It is clear that not only the special, deliberate and formal decrees of the magisterium, but also the 'everyday' teachings of the ordinary magisterium are to be received by the faithful in a spirit of meekness and docility, without questioning and without repining. As many a theologian disciplined by the Vatican can testify to his cost, whatever lip-service may be paid to the *sensus fidei* (the intuition of the truth) of the faithful and to the supreme authority of conscience, when the chips are down the modern Roman Catholic Church insists that the role of the faithful is to *receive*, not in any sense to *decide*, or even to share in decision-making. The most that even Congar, a passionate advocate of reception, can claim for it is that it gives 'credibility' to the teaching of the magisterium.[5]

---

[3] *Lumen gentium*, 25: W.M. Abbott, (ed.), *The Documents of Vatican II* (London and Dublin: Geoffrey Chapman, 1966), p. 48.

[4] *Catechism of the Catholic Church* (London: Geoffrey Chapman, 1994), pp. 441f. (2037–40).

[5] Y. Congar, 'Reception as an Ecclesiological Reality', in G. Alberigo and A. Weiler (eds), *Election and Consensus in the Church* (New York: Herder and Herder, 1972), p. 68.

This is a highly idealistic and actually ideological view of reception. Though stated in Vatican II and in the *Catechism* in an impressive and noble way, it neither fits the facts of church history nor squares with the divisions that continue within the whole Christian Church over doctrine and morals. While the authorities of the Roman Catholic Church state these claims for themselves with an air of lofty assurance, as though they were self-evident, the Eastern, Anglican and Protestant churches demur. They do not accept a number of Roman Catholic dogmas and they do not concur with Roman Catholic moral teaching in several respects. It is not that Orthodox, Anglicans and Protestants think faith and morals to be unimportant, or that they do not have their own principles and structures of authority (albeit in most cases less rigid ones). It is simply that they do not accept the Roman Catholic magisterium's specific claims for its own authority. They believe that their stance is vindicated by the facts of history.

Several scholars have explored recently the reception, over decades and even centuries, of the decisions of the early ecumenical councils. They have shown that their reception was a protracted, chequered and unpredictable process.[6] In relation to ecumenical councils we can be sure that the Church Fathers who promulgated their decrees expected them to be received and obeyed. But the fact that, even in the case of major councils – Nicaea (325), Constantinople (381), Ephesus (431), and Chalcedon (451) – this was often far from being a straightforward process, even when the sanctions of the state were deployed in their support, calls into question the viability of a 'top-down', hierarchical understanding of reception. Henry Chadwick points out that 'there are no great councils in the history of the Church

---

[6] H. Chadwick, 'Reception', in C. Sugden and V. Samuel, (eds), *Christian Life and Witness* (London: SPCK, 1997). Congar, 'Reception as an Ecclesiological Reality'.

whose decisions have not been subject to a process of critical assimilation or indeed . . . rejection'. Nicaea did not resolve the christological question but simply generated more debate. Chalcedon produced a 'huge conflagration'.[7] The history of the reception of general councils raises issues of timescale, the provisionality of conciliar decisions and the place of active discernment on the part of the faithful.

Moreover, the hierarchical construction of reception does not fit several of its other modern, ecumenical contexts.

- The term 'reception' is now applied to the mutual assimilation of ecumenical dialogues (such as the *Final Report* of the Anglican–Roman Catholic International Commission) by two or more churches or communions that have reached a new understanding of one another.[8]
- 'Reception' also refers to the way in which the creative contribution of an individual theologian who is of universal significance (Barth or Rahner perhaps) becomes absorbed into the bloodstream of the Church.
- Reception is also applied to the way in which the treasures of one tradition come to be shared with others. The hymns of Charles Wesley and the spirituality of the Moravians are cases in point. The papal ministry of universal primacy is a more controversial example, but responses to John Paul II's Encyclical *Ut Unum Sint* and to the ARCIC report *The Gift of Authority* may show that there is potential for carefully defined aspects of this primacy to be received in informal ways.[9]

---

[7] Chadwick, 'Reception', pp. 207–9.

[8] See e.g. J. Willebrands, 'The Ecumenical Dialogue and its Reception', *One in Christ* 21 (1985): 217–25. C.E. Clifford, 'Reception of the *Final Report*: Beyond Strengthened Agreement', *One in Christ* 32 (1996): 130–48.

[9] On *Ut Unum Sint* (1995) see *May They All Be One: A Response of the House of Bishops of the Church of England to* Ut Unum Sint (London: Church House Publishing, 1997). On *The Gift of Authority* (London: CTC; Toronto: Anglican Book Centre; New York: Church Publishing, 1999), see P. Fisher (ed), *Unpacking the Gift* (London: Church House Publishing, 2002).

- Reception is now used in a particularly broad sense of the way in which two churches may gravitate towards each other and, through theological dialogue and various forms of practical interaction, may 'receive' each other as churches through some form of mutual recognition.[10]

What is striking in all these cases is that the process of reception is marked by gradualness, mutuality, active discernment, responsibility, unpredictability and the real possibility of non-reception. These characteristics all register on the informal, personal and relational end of the scale of reception. They point to the only possible way in which one may make one's own what offers itself from elsewhere. Here we are on very different territory to that of the official Roman Catholic view of reception, the meek, obedient reception of what is handed down on authority.

It is this broader, more informal and flexible model of reception that I now want to explore in relation to Anglicanism. There are several substantial Anglican discussions of the concept of reception.[11] However, these are all concerned with the issue of ecumenical reception, rather than with the reception of developments within Anglicanism itself. It is precisely within Anglicanism, and specifically within the Church of England, that the idea of reception has undergone a further twist.

---

[10] J.M.R. Tillard, 'Reception – Comunion', *One in Christ* 28 (1992): 307–22. G. Gros, 'Reception and Roman Catholicism for the 1990s', *One in Christ* 31 (1995): 295–328.
[11] Chadwick, 'Reception'. G.R. Evans, *Method in Ecumenical Theology* (Cambridge: Cambridge University Press, 1996), ch.7. R. Greenacre, 'Two Aspects of Reception', in G.R. Evans (ed.), *Christian Authority: Essays in Honour of Henry Chadwick* (Oxford: Clarendon Press, 1998). N. Sagovsky, *Ecumenism, Christian Origins and the Practice of Communion* (Cambridge: Cambridge University Press, 2000).

An Open Process of Reception

The notion of reception becomes somewhat redefined when a church authority takes a decision that is then implemented in the life of that church *and at the same time explicitly sets it in the context of 'an open process of reception'*. This is precisely what the Church of England, endorsed by Resolution III.2 of the 1998 Lambeth Conference, has done in relation to the decision of the General Synod in 1992 to provide for the ordination of women to the presbyterate. The paradox of a formal decision within an open process raises a number of questions and has puzzled many. What is meant here?

It is clear from the documentation of the 1992 legislation and of the Episcopal Ministry Act of Synod 1993 that the model of reception that is being deployed here is not hierarchical or 'top-down'. It does not have connotations of inevitable acceptance by the faithful of a decision made by the appropriate authority (in this case the General Synod with the approval of Parliament). Rather the model is one of dialogue, mutuality and provisionality. In this documentation, as in the reports of the Eames Commission,[12] the process of reception is placed in the framework of communion (*koinonia*). Reception is thus not construed juridically but relationally. It is understood not as a political device for containing conflict, but as a spiritual reality that is endemic in the life of the Church. It is as though the Church of England has seen that reception is an inescapable ecclesial principle, one that needs to be acknowledged, owned and worked with. That church has recognized that major changes in the life of the Church and its ministry cannot be imposed by fiat, but require space and generosity and a certain amount of elasticity. Reception is seen as an

---

[12] *Being in Communion* (GS Misc. 418) (London: General Synod of the Church of England, 1993). *The Eames Commission: The Official Reports* (Toronto: Anglican Book Centre, 1994).

aspect of communion, as a dynamic of giving and receiving, a partnership in the gospel (cf. Philippians 1.5) between all who have a stake in the issue that needs to be resolved.

The open process of reception that the Church of England has embraced with respect to the ordination of women to the presbyterate makes sense against the background of Anglican ecclesiology. According to the Preface to the Declaration of Assent (Canon C15 1(1)), the Church of England regards itself as 'part of the One, Holy, Catholic and Apostolic Church', not the whole of it. In Canon A1 it affirms that it 'belongs to the true and apostolic Church of Christ', thus implying that the Church of Christ is something greater than itself. A church that confesses that, though a true church, it is not the whole Church, is bound by its nature to seek some kind of ecumenical consensus for any actions that seem to widen the rifts within Christendom.

Having said that, the churches in their state of separation must conduct themselves responsibly. They cannot be paralysed by inaction simply because the whole Church cannot act together and as one. When has that ever been the case? Moreover, it is sometimes inevitable that a part of the Church will take a decision that plays into the existing divisions between the various parts of the Church. Every time the Church of England legislates for its life and mission it exacerbates the situation of separation between itself and the Roman Catholic Church (not to mention other Christian ecclesial traditions). When it makes canon law, it does not seek the approval of the Pope (who can and does promulgate canon law unilaterally for the Roman Catholic Church). When it authorizes a new set of liturgical texts it does not submit them for approval to the Vatican, as local Roman Catholic bishops' conferences have to do. Rome does not appoint the bishops of the Anglican Communion and they do not do obeisance to the Pope (entering into 'hierarchical communion') as a condition of their episcopal ministry. The claims of the Roman Catholic Church with regard to the papacy are still claims of universal, ordinary and immediate jurisdiction over all dioceses, bishops, clergy and faithful laity throughout the world. (Needless to say, these claims are not accepted by the churches of the Anglican Communion, or by the Eastern Orthodox and Oriental Orthodox churches, or by the Old Catholic, Lutheran, Reformed, Methodist, Baptist and other churches.)

The Reformation itself is the most striking example of the need for part (or parts) of the Church to take responsibility for the reform of its life even when it cannot carry the whole Church with it. It was a central plank of the Reformation platform that, where crucial matters of salvation are concerned, where the conscience of Christian people is being harmed, a particular church has the right to take action, unilaterally if necessary, and indeed is bound to do so. We can see from the documentation of the period that the Reformation involved a set of emerging decisions that were offered precisely for an open, ecumenical process of reception. The innumerable polemical exchanges, academic disputations, formal hearings and colloquies, together with the constant Protestant appeals to a free and properly representative general council, surely demonstrate conclusively that, without compromising their convictions, the Reformers did indeed offer their various reforms for an open process of reception. Though this is seldom recognized, the Reformation was shot through with issues of reception.[13]

That stance, held by the Church of England and other reformed churches in the sixteenth century and not repudiated since, does not mean that the Church of England (or any other church for that matter) believes that it has the right to devise new doctrines. No church claims that right,

[13] See extensively on the Reformation and conciliarity P. Avis, *Anglicanism and the Christian Church: Theological Resources in Historical Perspective*, revised and expanded edition (Edinburgh: T&T Clark/Continuum, 2002), part 1.

not even the Roman Catholic Church. Every Christian church claims to hold fast to the trust deeds of Christianity, 'the faith once for all delivered to the saints' (Jude 1.3), the apostolic deposit of faith. But it does mean that the Church of England accepts that there is an imperative to articulate and to express apostolic doctrine in every specific context, both of time and of place. Doctrine needs to be embodied in practice, and for that to happen church decisions are necessary. A decision to maintain the status quo – though an option in some circumstances – is no less a decision than a decision to make a change in a church's practice.

Reception, Tradition and Mission

Discerning the truth of change in the Church raises the question of the relation of reception to tradition. Several writers on reception point to the language of 'handing on' and 'receiving' in the New Testament (e.g. 1 Corinthians 11.23; 15.1–3). Receiving and conferring are two sides of the same coin. You cannot receive something unless it is offered to you. 'What do you have that you have not received?' (1 Corinthians 4.7). Receiving is an act of appropriation of what is being held out to us. What God has given is in the first place his love and because of his love he has given us his Son (John 3.16). We have 'received' Jesus Christ himself (Colossians 2.6) in the act of receiving his gospel (1 Corinthians 15.1; Galatians 1.9–12).[14] Tradition is the *given* pole of what is being transmitted. Reception is the *active* pole. What is handed on does not remain unaffected or unchanged by the process. It is adapted, embodied, subject to practice and to context. The act of appropriation makes a difference. It is a complete illusion to imagine that the life of the Early Church can be replicated or reproduced unchanged in our very different

[14] Cf. J. Zizioulas, 'The Theological Problem of Reception', *One in Christ* 21 (1985): 190.

(but not necessarily superior) times and culture. The process of reception always sets the issue in a new light, one way or the other.

It is sometimes suggested that the very idea of reception was invented by the Church of England to extricate it from a difficulty – the problem of wilfully persisting with the ordination of women without a sufficient consensus. Such a cynical suggestion could only be put forward in ignorance of church history. Reception is a permanent feature of the life of the Christian Church. It belongs to its nature as catholic and apostolic. As the Spirit-guided Body of Christ, the Church is continually developing its fundamental appropriation of the apostolic faith in order to respond to fresh circumstances. To meet new knowledge, fresh insights and changes in society, the Church draws deeply on the apostolic faith, on the resources of biblical truth. Reception is, therefore, related both to the demands of apostolic continuity and to the inculturation of the faith. Since the Church's context is always a mission context, reception is an essentially missiological concept. It is grounded in the spiritual vitality of the Church as the Spirit-bearing body. In reception the Church is inevitably involved in an ongoing process of assimilation and discernment, changing in such a way that it reaches out in mission to the humanity that Christ came to redeem, while at the same time remaining utterly faithful to its apostolic foundation. Reception is then essentially the contextual – but critical – application of the Christian faith.[15]

On this model, it is the nature of reception to be exploratory. It is open, not in the sense that anything can happen, but in the sense of being open-ended, not forestalling the outcome. A real act of discernment and of

---

[15] This idea is slightly differently applied by Zizioulas, 'The Theological Problem of Reception', p. 189.

judgement is called for, and this could go either way.[16] The verdict is not assumed. Reception in its Anglican (or perhaps I should say, non-Roman Catholic) sense is a neutral term. Despite a common misapprehension to the contrary, it does not imply that ultimately a particular development will be positively accepted as God's will for the Church. No sense of an inevitable outcome should be imported into the ecumenical concept of reception. We can see this from the various uses mentioned above. We cannot, I think, assume that the work of ARCIC on authority in the Church, culminating most recently in *The Gift of Authority*, will get a positive response when it has been fully studied and reflected on. It is possible that it may be seen as a basically unhelpful approach, or at least as a 'curate's egg'. Similarly, it is by no means certain that the wider Church will want to endorse the distinctive theological emphases of Karl Barth or Karl Rahner, though it is surely bound to learn something from them both.

It is, therefore, clearly implied in the open process of the reception of the decision of the Church of England to provide for the ordination of women that the decision could be reappraised. In other words, it is hypothetically reversible. If the General Synod were so minded, it could change its canons to the *status quo ante* 1993, with the result that no more women would be ordained priest after that point. Those already ordained would work out their ministry to its conclusion without calling into question, in a canonical sense, the validity of their priestly ministry. It is not the ordinations (orders) of individual women clergy that is subject to the process of open reception. They are duly and canonically ordained and are on a par with their male counterparts. Neither Resolutions A and B (provided in the

---

[16] See D. Brown, '*Phronesis*, Development and Doctrinal Definition', *International Journal for the Study of the Christian Church* 1 (2001): 70–85.

original 1992 legislation for the Ordination of Women), nor the provisions for Extended Episcopal Oversight of the Episcopal Ministry Act of Synod itself, call that in question. These provisions are there to provide space within the Church of England for those who in conscience believe that that church has acted wrongly in introducing women priests.

It is a firm principle that a church has the authority to ordain those whom it considers fit subjects for ordination. When so ordained they are truly ordained. No individual or group has the power to decide that other individuals or groups within the same church are not ordained. As Canon A4 says, those who have been duly ordained according to the ordination rites of the Church of England 'are lawfully ... ordained ..., and ought to be accounted, both by themselves and others, to be truly bishops, priests or deacons'. To attempt to drive a wedge in terms of validity between the orders of Anglican male clergy and those of Anglican female clergy is counter-productive. It falls foul of Pope Leo XIII's condemnation of Anglican orders in the Bull *Apostolicae curae* in 1896.[17] Anglican orders, male and female, stand or fall together. The same ecclesial authority stands behind both. That is why it is vital to insist that it is the synodical decision, not the ministry of individual women, that is subject to a process of open reception.[18] Unless we take seriously the hypothetical but genuine possibility that the synodical decision could be reversed (setting aside for the moment any strong personal convictions that we may hold to the contrary), we have not grasped the crucial point about an open process of reception.

---

[17] See P. Avis, *Anglican Orders and the Priesting of Women* (London: Darton, Longman & Todd, 1998).

[18] As Mary Tanner soundly insists: 'Reception and Provisionality among Anglicans', *Mid-Stream* 29 (1990): 55–61, esp. 59.

Reception as Discernment

The key to understanding reception in this sense is the notion of *discernment*. Reception involves a process of study and evaluation in which the truth (or otherwise) of a development is tested and discerned. This is an act of spiritual evaluation and judgement, in which the Church waits prayerfully on the leading of the Holy Spirit. Reception/discernment is a pneumatological event: we look to the Spirit to guide us. Now the Spirit, though given to every baptized Christian, is primarily given to the Church as the Body of Christ. The Spirit is present corporately. If we invoke the Spirit to guide us in reception/discernment, we have to acknowledge that this is not an individual matter. Reception does not operate at the individual level. It is not a synonym for 'the right of private judgement'. It is only as we are bound together with others through baptism, the foundational sacrament of initiation into the Body of Christ, that we can participate in a process of reception. Reception/discernment is an action that we can only undertake as we are bound together in Christ.

This process of discernment is bound to take place not only before any decision is made, but also afterwards. A formal process of reception/discernment – one launched, for example, by the General Synod – normally implies that an informal process of reception/discernment has been under way for some time previously. A certain momentum of conviction has built up. There is a ground-swell of support for a particular development. This was certainly the case in the Church of England with regard to the ordination of women. But to know when the time is right for a critical decision to be taken, and thus for an informal process of reception/discernment to become a formal process, is a fine judgement. In this respect, 'ripeness is all'. Opinions will vary as to whether that ripeness, that sense of the fullness of time, that gathering of consensus, had been attained in

1992 when a sufficient majority in the General Synod voted for the ordination of women.

The true nature of reception, as a process of spiritual discernment, is brought out when we acknowledge the truth that the eventual outcome of the process is known only to God. It is hidden in the mysterious eternal purpose of God, centred in Christ (Ephesians 1.10). Theologically, it is set within an eschatological framework. We may think that we can glimpse the end afar off and we may or may not be right. But, nevertheless, we journey in faith; we do not have guarantees (cf. 2 Corinthians 5.7; Hebrews 11.13). To participate actively in a corporate process of reception/discernment is, therefore, an act of faith. It calls for the exercise of the Christian virtues. The language of 'integrity' that has been much invoked around the issue of the ordination of women in the Church of England is entirely appropriate. Integrity, humility and spiritual maturity are the qualities needed in order to handle profound and contentious issues (cf. 1 Corinthians 2.6–16).

Ecumenical Reception

The Episcopal Ministry Act of Synod 1993 (GS 1085) urged all concerned to endeavour to ensure that 'discernment in the wider Church of the rightness or otherwise of the Church of England's decision to ordain women to the priesthood should be as open a process as possible'. The idea of an open process of reception brings home the fact that reception is not the concern of any one church or world communion. It belongs in a fully ecumenical context. Reception is a matter for the whole Church. Gifts and insights, wisdom and vision need to be shared. All Christians are gifted with the *sensus fidei*, the faculty of spiritual discernment that shapes the process of reception. *Lumen Gentium* calls it a 'supernatural sense of faith', imparted by the Holy Spirit, that means that 'the body of the faithful as a whole cannot err in matters of belief'.[19]

The decision of the Church of England — a church that explicitly acknowledges that it forms only a part of the one, holy, catholic and apostolic Church — with regard to the ordination of women in a divided universal Church entails that reception must take place on an ecumenical basis. Any Christian church, and especially the Church of England (and by the same token all the other churches of the Anglican Communion), is honour-bound to seek ecumenical agreement before making such a change to its polity as the ordination of women. It is in the nature of any partial expression of the Church to seek to be conformed to the whole. Sadly, we seldom see this principle being observed by the two largest churches of Christendom, the Roman Catholic and the Eastern Orthodox, because they actually regard themselves as the only truly authentic expressions of the one Church. But we do not always see it where we expect to see it — in churches such as the Methodist Church that, like the Anglican churches, confess that they are part of a larger whole. However, where this broader perspective is acknowledged, it suggests that, while there is certainly a place for vision, there is also a need for restraint. The ultimate context of a process of open reception is the full visible unity of the Christian Church. Reception is predicated on the reality that the Church is currently divided over a number of important issues of belief and practice, of which the ordination of women comprises only one, but that it is essentially one in Christ and is called to make that unity visible. So with regard to the ordination of women, a mission imperative may seem to pull one way; a unity imperative may seem to pull the other way.

---

[19] *Lumen gentium*, 2.12: Abbott (ed.), p. 29. The pioneering work on the *sensus fidei* is of course J.H. Newman, *On Consulting the Faithful in Matters of Doctrine*, ed. J. Coulson, (London: Geoffrey Chapman, 1961).

Differentiated Consensus

While unfamiliar expressions of faith and practice are being tested, the interaction of differing, even opposing points of view plays a vital part. Therefore, minorities have a special importance in holding open the possibility of a fundamental rethink on the part of a church. When they bear witness to their minority convictions with courtesy and charity (a courtesy and charity that, we trust, mirrors the identical qualities manifested by the dominant majority) they have a right to be heard. When they argue their case on well thought-out theological and pastoral grounds they give added weight to their concerns. More than that: the Church needs to hear their voice. We cannot discern the truth without one another. A condition of hearing the 'still, small voice' of God (cf. 2 Kings 19.12 AV) is that we are open and vulnerable towards those within our fellowship who believe differently. Christ's truth will not be revealed to me if I imagine that I can hear it without listening with my sister and my brother. In the Royal Priesthood of the baptized, all the Lord's people are prophets (1 Peter 2.9; cf. Numbers 11.29; Joel 2. 28f.). We have to reckon with the possibility that a prophetic word may be given to the Church through those with whom we happen to disagree profoundly.

A patient process of reception allows for the possibility of the *sensus fidei* coming together into a *consensus fidelium*, a consensus of the faithful. Within the process of reception, a consensus that points in one particular direction or another may begin to emerge. At this stage, where there is some recognition of common concerns but no resolution of the issue, views may exist side by side in a 'directional plurality'. Consensus should not attempt to be exclusive – if it does, it is no longer consensus but the dictatorship of the majority – but it should always and as a matter of principle make space for the possibility of dissent. Participants to the debate should feel able to put all their cards on the table. No position should be despised or treated with contempt. The state of play at this stage represents a 'differentiated consensus' in which certain concerns are shared, there are some agreed points, and some ground rules for discussion and debate are generally accepted, but the basic issue of principle remains unresolved.[20] The notion of 'differentiated consensus' allows us to do justice to the twin realities that have to be faced: the reality of partial agreement and the reality of partial disagreement; common ground and diverging convictions; unity and disunity. Inevitably some boundaries will be drawn for the sake of distinctness and to provide mutual support, but these should not be erected into walls with no portals.

We should also reckon with the fact that there will be different perceptions of what is actually happening in the process of reception. The process is dynamic and relational (not cerebral and confrontational) in its nature, and the leading issues may develop or assume different proportions. We need to be receptive to the distinctive logic of the engagement, mindful that it is a personal and relational logic, not an abstract and theoretical one. Given that sensitivity, reception as a process of discernment can lead to a new 'translation' where we find a new language with which to address one another. As a result, the issues can begin to look rather different. This sort of development can point to degrees of agreement and degrees of visible communion that correspond to that graduated agreement.

Reception and Communion

Effective reception presupposes a certain milieu, a qualitative ecology, with regard to the relation to one another of Christians who are engaged in the process of reception/

---

[20] See on this concept the chapter by William G. Rusch in this volume.

discernment. Reception cannot happen without communion. It is *koinonia* that undergirds and sustains the process of reception/discernment, as it does all authentic dynamics of ecclesial existence. As Sagovsky suggests, it is the central reality of the Christian life, indeed of all life.[21] *Koinonia* is grounded in baptism.[22] In baptism we are placed by the Holy Spirit into the Body of Christ (1 Corinthians 12.13). We are thus made one both with Christ, the Head of the Body, and with all the members. We cannot have the one without the other. We cannot distance ourselves from the members without impairing our fellowship with Christ our Head. Our unity with God, Father, Son and Holy Spirit, is the very same unity that unites us with our fellow Christians (1 John 1.3f.). Those with different views, passionately held, are all bound together in the baptized Body. That is no doubt how the Good Lord designed that his Church should be. He did not foresee unanimity, comfortable consensus and the absence of conflict. The New Testament gives no encouragement to that idea – quite the contrary. Sagovsky writes: 'Conflict is integral to life in community. It is not the presence of conflict that is unhealthy for communal life, but the premature suppression of conflict in the interests of an inauthentic unity.'[23] Jesus intended that his disciples should wrestle with truth in all humility and learn from one another. As Sagovsky has so helpfully brought out with reference to the dialogues of Plato, *koinonia* involves dialogue.[24] The way that Christians handle that process is almost more important than the conclusions they arrive at. They are bound together on the Way (*sunhodos*).

If reception is primarily the process of waiting upon the

[21] Sagovsky, *Ecumenism*, p. 2.

[22] See further P. Avis, *Christians in Communion* (London: Geoffrey Chapman/ Mowbray, 1990), ch. 2.

[23] Sagovsky, *Ecumenism*, p. 8. On conflict in the Church see also S.W. Sykes, *The Identity of Christianity* (London: SPCK, 1984).

[24] Sagovsky, *Ecumenism*, pp. 9f. and ch. 3.

Holy Spirit at work within the Body to enable the discernment of truth, we cannot participate in the process unless we remain in the Body. To switch to the equivalent Johannine metaphor, the branches only remain attached to the Vine while they remain attached to each other (John 15.1–11). That mutual abiding or indwelling is above all *eucharistic*. As Zizioulas argues, the Eucharist is the definitive context of reception.[25] It is as we are united in the Eucharist that we are open to the Spirit's brooding over the Body of Christ, breathing on it (cf. Genesis 1.2 AV; John 20.22). To breach eucharistic fellowship, as some have done, is to damage the process of reception and hamper the leading of the Spirit. The Eames Commission was right to warn that no-one should say that they are out of communion with those views they may oppose. That wisdom is reinforced if we consider that to put ourselves out of communion is to put ourselves outside the process of reception, and to put ourselves outside the process of reception is to put ourselves outside the sphere of the Spirit's guiding.

An Anglican understanding of reception places great weight on the corporate, organic understanding of the Church. It points to the idea of a Church listening to itself, listening to the Spirit within it and listening and responding to minority voices within it, before making the portentous judgement that the *consensus fidelium* on a contentious issue has been attained. That does not mean that the Church is paralysed and unable to take decisions, but it does mean weighing the moment very carefully, honouring the consciences of those who reject the consensus and bending over backwards to accommodate their concerns, without putting a time limit on that 'economy'.[26] It was a

[25] Zizioulas, 'The Theological Problem of Reception', pp. 191ff.

[26] Cf. Greenacre, 'Two Aspects of Reception', p.41 and my chapter 'The Episcopal Ministry Act of Synod 1993: A "Bearable Anomaly" ', in this volume.

Roman Catholic, though not a typical one, Lord Acton, who said: 'The test of liberty is the position and security of minorities.'[27]

[27] R. Hill, *Lord Acton* (New Haven and London: Yale University Press, 2000), p. 216, citing H. Paul (ed.), *Letters of Lord Acton to Mary, Daughter of the Right Hon. W.E. Gladstone*, 2nd edn (London, 1913), p. 53.

39

3

RECEPTION AND COMMUNION

John Hind

This chapter is about reception and communion, and the relevance of these themes to current debates and divisions over the ordination of women to the priesthood.[1] After a general introduction, there is a brief consideration of the nature of the language of Christian faith and its corporate character. This leads to reflection on the *sensus fidei* and its relation to the *sensus fidelium* and the question of mutual recognizability. Immediately this raises questions about how we recognize each other and how extensive that recognition has to be if we are to be confident that we genuinely hold the apostolic faith. Relevant here are the notions of development in doctrine (especially as regards diachronic unity) and the hierarchy of truths – perhaps in its guise as a discussion about fundamentals and *adiaphora* – (as regards synchronic unity). For those who believe that the faith has been uniquely revealed and that it has to be proclaimed afresh in each generation, there must be a double presumption that doctrine both develops and remains the same.

How developments occur and how they should be evaluated is a problem in a divided Church. The particular kind of unity described as 'communion' is not so much the fruit of agreement and insight as the precondition for them. Hence the danger of innovation when Christians do not live in communion (full visible unity) with each other. New

[1] Questions about women and the episcopate are not treated in this paper. This way of stating the matter is not to prejudge whether this is a separate issue or not.

grounds for remaining divided emerge, which go beyond those which caused the original schism.

Separated denominations have a double problem here. On the one hand, they must usually behave as if they were the whole Church. The Christian life cannot always be lived looking over one's shoulder to what others are doing. We have to be able to be confident that the faith as we have received it is authentically the apostolic faith, and that the way of life we live can be genuinely graced by and pleasing to God. On the other hand, the divisions in the Church are real enough and are part of the ecclesial reality we have received. (We may not agree with everything in the faith and practice of other Christians, but we do have to be able to account for them.) This should lead us to cherish what we have in common, and especially those elements that most bind the body together, both within our own ecclesial family and within the whole Church. The degree of freedom a particular church or denomination has to develop its own way of doing things must depend primarily on the centrality of the issue in question to the fundamentals of the faith. In evaluating our own and others' practice we have to acknowledge the pressure particular churches experience within their own cultural environments to shape their presentation of the common faith and their handling of some second order issues in ways which enable them to give authentic Christian witness there and then. It should be noted that these points apply just as much to churches divided by geography as they do to churches divided by confession.

Reception, Recognition and Communion

'Reception' and 'communion' are big words. 'Reception' refers primarily to the process by which we receive the

[2] Strictly speaking of course, 'reception' refers to the process of 'having received' the faith. That is to say, we should not really use the term until the process is complete. Of this more later.

faith[2] – and ultimately, of course, in the words of the Prologue to St John's Gospel, to how the world does (or does not) receive the Word, who was with God from the beginning and who was coming into the world. 'Communion' refers to our fellowship with God in Christ and with those who have proclaimed the gospel to us. Two classic texts illustrate an intrinsic theological link between reception and communion. 'To all who received him, who believed in his name, he gave power to become children of God'[3] and 'What we have seen and heard we proclaim also to you, so that you may have fellowship with us; and our fellowship is with the Father and with his Son Jesus Christ.'[4]

We notice that reception means reception of the gospel and what pertains to it, and that communion is ultimately communion with God. It is essential to keep these horizons in view and not to allow their scope to be restricted to merely contingent questions of epistemology or sociology. (This is particularly important if we are to reassure some sceptics who believe that the appeal to reception in the Church of England today is simply a highfalutin euphemism for eliminating dissent over the ordination of women and for driving the opposition out.)

In John 1 the Word is described as the one through whom all things were made and who enlightens everyone. Yet, despite this, when 'he came to his own, his own did not receive him'. Not receiving in this context implies not recognizing, and so we can see that recognition and non-recognition are closely related to reception in this fundamental sense. If the faith once received brings us into fellowship and when maintained preserves us in fellowship, we shall be able to recognize those with whom we are in fellowship partly on the basis of their having received the same faith.

[3] John 1.12.
[4] 1 John 1.3.

This, of course, raises questions about how we recognize each other and how extensive mutual recognition has to be if we are to be confident that we genuinely hold the apostolic faith together. It must be stressed that this is not the same thing as insisting on complete agreement on everything. Agreeing to differ in areas where disagreement is tolerable and identifying what those areas are is as much part of mutual recognition as is unanimity.

Nevertheless, differences may be barriers to recognition, and their existence thus provides a challenge to identify criteria and methods for discernment. When distances of time or place lead Christian communities to acquire or develop characteristic emphases, these methods become particularly important. The relevance of this in the case of separated Christian confessions should be apparent. It is no less relevant to a denomination like the Church of England and most other member churches of the Anglican Communion in which the mutual recognizability of each other as sharing the same faith is under some strain.

The Word of God and the sensus fidei

If God's definitive answer to the questions, 'God, who are you?', 'God, where are you?' and most fundamentally of course, 'God, are you?' is Jesus Christ, the eternal Word made flesh, then any words about God or God's incarnate Word are secondary. Theological and doctrinal formulae are 'words about the Word', attempts in human language to express the inexpressible. At the same time, the very fact of the Incarnation justifies the attempt and reassures us that, although they are bound to be inadequate, our words are not *a priori* illegitimate. The reason is that the 'flesh' assumed by the Word includes human language.

Christians might be expected to take two things for granted in this regard. First, as it is through the Word that all things were made, and because that same Word enlightens every one, there is a certain affinity between humankind and God that enables human beings in virtue of their humanness to be able to recognize and say something about God. Second, however, because the eternal Word became flesh, with all that implies of a particular life in a particular place and a particular time, whatever this 'universal' human speech says about God has to be authenticated uniquely by reference to this one person, Jesus Christ.

A further principle follows from these. Our ability to be confident in what we say about God is related not only to our common humanity, made in the image of God, and to the unique authentication of that in Jesus Christ, but also to our relationship with Jesus Christ today. Another way of putting this is to say that the incarnation of the Word makes it possible for the lives of those who are 'in Christ' to be themselves what we might call 'secondary authentications' of human God-talk.

Both these ideas: that of common humanity and that of being 'in Christ' are essentially corporate notions. We recognize, receive, know and speak as individuals, but only in fellowship, that is to say 'in communion', bearing in mind that the Christian term communion always means fellowship with one another and with God in and through Christ who is the focus and guarantee of our knowledge of God. All this leads to the important concept of a *sensus fidei* possessed by members of the Church.

Sensus fidei is not the same as *sensus fidelium* or *consensus fidelium*, although it is closely related to these concepts.[5] *Sensus fidei* refers to a supernatural gift of faith which creates in the believer a kind of faculty for discerning what is and what is not in accordance with the faith, and hence for recognizing those who share it. This faculty may be in better or worse repair, partly as a result of the care Christian

---

[5] Cf. J. Tillard, '*Consensus fidelium*' in N. Lossky et al. (eds), *Dictionary of the Ecumenical Movement* (Geneva: WCC, 1991), pp. 225f.

communities and individuals take with the faith and the influences that might strengthen or weaken it. Distractions, habitual sins and addictions of all sorts can dull or distort this internal awareness; while the practice of virtue, accompanied by the baptismal habit of repentance, can help it remain keen.[6]

Of course, we are all backsliders, and for this reason if for no other the *sensus fidei*, while held by individuals (groups do not have feelings!) is in practice a corporate faculty. To speak of a *sensus fidelium* or a *consensus fidelium* is not to imply that truth is determined by a majority vote, but is a claim that for the possession and discernment of truth we need the confirmation of our sisters and brothers in the faith.

An evocative mechanism in the Early Church for sustaining the corporate synchronic and diachronic unity of Christians in the faith was the liturgical and catechetical practice of the *traditio* and *redditio symboli*. During Lent the bishop would teach (hand over) the creed to the catechumens who returned the following week to recite (hand back) what they had learnt.[7] In this way the faith is passed on from one generation to another and receives its echo.

Securus iudicat orbis terrarum[8] means more than 'safety in numbers'. It is by way of an explication of the Lord's promise that the Holy Spirit would lead his disciples into the

---

[6] I am indebted in this section of the paper to a recent reading of S. Fowl, *Engaging Scripture* (Oxford: Blackwell, 1999).

[7] Cf. Augustine, *de Symbolo* 11: 'Today week you will have to repeat what you have learnt today. Your godparents are responsible for teaching you ... no one need be nervous and so fail to repeat the words. Do not worry, I am your father. I do not carry a strap or cane like a schoolmaster.' Translation in E. Yarnold, *The Awe Inspiring Rites of Initiation* (Slough: St Paul Publications, 1971), p. 13.

[8] Augustine, *C. Ep. Parm.* II. 4. 24. The whole sentence reads: 'Securus iudicat orbis terrarum bonos non esse qui se dividunt ab orbe terrarum in quacunque parte terrarum.' In the context of his dispute with Donatism, Augustine is arguing that the Church in every place needs to retain its sense of the whole. The argument can be applied *mutatus mutandis* to 'denominations'. The basic point holds good, even if the fact of denominational identity indicates that the horse has already bolted.

whole truth; it was a promise made to them together. At the same time, he promised that the Spirit would remind them of all he had taught them. This is a further reason why *sensus fidei* should never be interpreted as 'mass (even mass Christian) opinion'. It also presupposes the mutual indwelling or 'abiding' of Christ and his disciples.

Reception and Development

Reception may be described as the way in which a doctrinal formulation comes to be recognized as 'at home' in the Christian community once it is accepted as being in conformity with the tradition. It is less clear whether it is appropriate to apply the term to liturgical, pastoral or disciplinary practices, except when these are inescapably linked to a matter of fidelity to the gospel.

The marriage of clergy may be taken to illustrate the point. Although clerical celibacy could scarcely be said to have been 'received' by the Church, if and when the Roman Catholic Church formally abandons this requirement the idea of married clergy will no doubt take some 'getting used to' in some quarters. This should not be confused with reception, since compulsory celibacy at least has not generally been regarded as a matter of fundamental doctrine. 'Getting used to' is quite the wrong register for reception, which refers to a more positive apprehension of the truth. Care needs to be taken therefore about the status of formulae or practices to which talk of a process of reception is appropriate.

Similarly, we should be somewhat wary of using the term until it is clear that a particular doctrinal formulation has in fact been received. This is because up to that point the formulation must be considered a theologoumenon, an opinion, even a conviction, which no matter how strongly held and felt to be convincing by individuals or particular churches, should not be affirmed to be essential to the faith until *orbis terrarum* has spoken. This of course brings us straight to the problem of decision-making and mutual recognition in a divided Church, because 'reception' has been shown to be an essentially conservative process.

On the other hand development must occur. It happens every time the gospel is preached, announced and expressed. Every time a preacher opens his or her mouth, he or she clothes the Word in new words. Most of these new formulations are ephemeral. But some become established, because they serve the needs of the Church in changing circumstances.

It is important to acknowledge the inevitability of development, while recognizing that this can lead to divisions. The decree *Unitatis redintegratio* on ecumenism of the Second Vatican Council puts the matter like this: 'the inheritance handed on by the apostles was received with differences of form and manner, and from the earliest times of the Church it was expressed variously in different places, owing to diversities of character and condition of life. All of this, quite apart from external causes, prepared the way for divisions arising also from a lack of mutual understanding and charity.'[9]

Accepting therefore that new formulations are constantly being made, of which some will prove necessary and be accepted as true (i.e. it is possible that they may be received), reception is not only conservative, it is also a process serving development.

Needless to say, none of this happens in a tidy or universal way. For example, a particular church[10] may feel itself led to an apparent innovation that may seem to its

---

[9] *Unitatis redintegratio*, 14 (text and translation: N.P. Tanner (ed.), *Decrees of the Ecumenical Councils* (London: Sheed & Ward; Georgetown University Press, 1990), vol. 2, p. 916.

[10] I am using the term 'particular churches' with deliberate ambiguity. Traditionally used to refer to dioceses or national churches, it may by extension apply to denominations.

own decision-making bodies or even the whole body of the faithful in that church justified or necessary or required by tradition, but which does not have the present assent of *orbis terrarum*. Because what is at stake is divine truth rather than the beliefs-system of a religious society, and because not all developments are true, churches like individual Christians should exercise due care in this matter.

In his *Essay on the Development of Christian Doctrine* John Henry Newman[11] set out seven 'distinctive tests between development and corruption'. It is worth noting the brief summaries he gives of each. 'The first test ... of a faithful or legitimate development is its *preservation of the essential idea* of the doctrine or polity which it represents.'[12] 'The *continuity or alteration of the principles* on which an idea has developed is a second mark of discrimination between a true development and a corruption.'[13] It is a power of assimilation or *unitive power* that constitutes the third characteristic of faithful developments.[14] 'Another evidence ... of the faithfulness of an ultimate development is its *definite anticipation* at an early period in the history of the idea to which it belongs.'[15] '*Logical sequence* ... is a fifth characteristic of developments, which are faithfully drawn from the ideas to which they profess to belong.'[16] 'A sixth test of a true development is its being *an addition which is conservative* of what has gone before it.'[17] And finally, 'while a corruption is distinguished from decay by its energetic action, it is distinguished from a development by its *transitory character*'.[18]

---

[11] J.H. Newman, *An Essay on the Development of Christian Doctrine* (1845 edn), ed. J. Cameron (London: Penguin, 1974), pp. 116–47 (I.III).

[12] Ibid., p. 124 (I.III.2).

[13] Ibid., p. 127 (I.III.3).

[14] Ibid., p. 133 (I.III.5).

[15] Ibid., p. 136 (I.III.6).

[16] Ibid., p. 141 (I.III.7).

[17] Ibid., p. 144 (I.III.8).

[18] Ibid., p. 147 (I.III.9).

Newman wrote his *Essay* in part to justify the notion of development in opposition to those who took an oversimple view of *sola Scriptura* or of tradition understood merely as 'deposit'.

Anglicans have in the past been somewhat neuralgic about what they perceive as innovations. In this they have been consistent with the arguments of many Church Fathers. Irenaeus,[19] Cyril of Jerusalem[20] and Vincent of Lerinum[21] had different concerns in their several genera-

---

[19] Irenaeus, *Adv. Haer.* I. 10. 2 (ANCL): 'The Church, having received this preaching and this faith, although scattered throughout the world, yet, as if occupying but one house, carefully preserves it. She also believes these points of doctrine just as if she had but one soul, and one and the same heart, and she proclaims them, and teaches them, and hands them down, with perfect harmony, as if she possessed only one mouth. For, although the languages of the world are dissimilar, yet the import of the tradition is one and the same. For the churches which have been planted in Germany do not believe or hand down anything different, nor do those in Spain, nor those in Gaul, nor those in the East, nor those in Egypt, nor those in Libya, nor those which have been established in the central regions of the world. But as the sun, that creature of God, is one and the same throughout the whole world, so also the preaching of the truth shines everywhere, and enlightens all men that are willing to come to a knowledge of the truth. Nor will any one of the rulers of the churches, however highly gifted he may be in point of eloquence, teach doctrines different from those (for no one is greater than the Master); nor, on the other hand, will he who is deficient in power of expression inflict injury on the tradition. For the faith being ever one and the same, neither does one who is able at great length to make discourse regarding it, make any addition to it, nor does one, who can say but little, diminish it.'

[20] Cyril of Jerusalem, *Cat. Or.* XVIII.23: 'The Church, Catholic or universal, gets her name from the fact that she is scattered throughout the whole world from one end of the earth to the other, and because she teaches universally and without omission all the doctrines which are to be made known to mankind, whether concerned with visible or invisible things, with heavenly or earthly things. Then again because she teaches one way of worship to all men, nobles or commoners, learned or simple; finally because she universally cures and heals every sort of sin which is committed by soul and body. Moreover there is in her every kind of virtue in words and deeds and spiritual gifts of every sort.'

[21] Cf. Vincent of Lerinum, *Comm.* II. 6: 'Moreover, in the Catholic Church itself, all possible care must be taken, that we hold that faith which has been believed everywhere, always, by all. For that is truly and in the strictest sense "Catholic," which, as the name itself and the reason of the thing declare,

tions, but all bore witness to the universality of what is to believed by Christians.

Athanasius had some particularly interesting observations on the difference between the way in which the Council of Nicaea spoke of disciplinary matters and its approach to dogmatic issues. Commenting on the resolution of the date of Easter and the condemnation of Arianism, he explains that,

> concerning Easter they wrote, 'It seemed good as follows,' for it did then seem good that there should be a general compliance; but about the faith they wrote not, 'It seemed good,' but, 'Thus believes the Catholic Church;' and thereupon they confessed how they believed, in order to shew that their own sentiments were not novel, but Apostolical; and what they wrote down was no discovery of theirs, but is the same as was taught by the Apostles.[22]

This distinction was also made by the English Reformers. We read in the Thirty-nine Articles,[23] of the Authority of the Church, that:

> The Church hath power to decree Rites or Ceremonies, and authority in Controversies of Faith: and yet it is not lawful for the Church to ordain any thing that is contrary to God's Word written, neither may it so expound one place of Scripture, that it be repugnant to another. Wherefore, although the Church be a witness and a keeper of Holy Writ, yet, as it ought not to decree any thing against the same, so besides the same ought it not to enforce any thing to be believed for necessity of Salvation.

This approach finds more recent support from a somewhat

---

comprehends all universally. This rule we shall observe if we follow universality, antiquity, consent. We shall follow universality if we confess that one faith to be true, which the whole Church throughout the world confesses; antiquity, if we in no wise depart from those interpretations which it is manifest were notoriously held by our holy ancestors and fathers; consent, in like manner, if in antiquity itself we adhere to the consentient definitions and determinations of all, or at the least of almost all priests and doctors.'

[22] Athanasius, *De synodis* 5.
[23] Article XX.

unexpected quarter. The dogmatic constitution *Pastor aeternus*[24] of the First Vatican Council is explicit on this point: 'The Holy Spirit was promised to the successors of Peter not so that they could, by his revelation, make known some new doctrine, but that, by his assistance, they might religiously guard and faithfully expound the revelation or deposit of faith transmitted by the apostles.'[25]

It is not my purpose here to attempt any evaluation of the Roman Catholic dogma of papal infallibility[26] according to the criteria I am outlining, instructive though that might be. I am more interested in the clarity with which the Constitution specifically excludes any 'new doctrine' from the scope of guarantee of infallibility.

Reception is the process whereby the whole Church sifts developments and discerns their rightness or otherwise. A development may be considered to have been 'received' when in matters essential to the foundations of the faith the whole Church may be deemed to have given its assent, or when the whole Church accepts that diversity on a particular matter may be legitimate. Christians believe this to be a Spirit-led process which will have some external identifying marks and methods, but which cannot be reduced to them. Security in faith requires that we should be able to

---

[24] *Pastor aeternus*, First Dogmatic Constitution on the Church of Christ, First Vatican Council, Session 4, 18 July 1870 (text and translation in Tanner, *Decrees*, vol. 2, pp. 811–16).

[25] *Pastor aeternus*, ch. 4, p. 816, lines 5–8: 'Neque enim Petri successoribus Spiritus sanctus promissus est, ut eo revelante novam doctrinam patefacerent, sed ut eo assistente traditam per apostolos revelationem seu fidei depositum sancte custodirent et fideliter exponerent.'

[26] *Pastor aeternus*, ch. 4, p. 816, lines 29–37: 'Definimus: Romanum pontificem, cum ex cathedra loquitur, id est, cum omnium christianorum pastoris et doctoris munere fungens, pro suprema sua apostolica auctoritate doctrinam de fide vel moribus ab universa ecclesia tenendam definit, per assistentiam divinam, ipsi in Petro promisam, ea infallibilitate pollere, qua divinus Redemptor ecclesiam suam in definienda doctrina de fide vel moribus instructam esse voluit; i deo eiusmodi Romani pontificis definitiones ex sese, non autem ex consensu ecclesiae irreformabiles esse.'

have confidence in the formulae through which faith is received and expressed; faith however implies that our security is in God and God's truth rather than in formulae.

This all suggests that the question of development and the reception of doctrine demands checks and balances if we are not either to fly off into an individualistic free-for-all or to reduce faith to mere assent to a set of propositions. These checks and balances include the need to distinguish between, on the one hand, the faith which is necessary for salvation and, on the other, either the formulae through which that faith is expressed or matters which may safely be left to local or individual judgement.

The more divided the Church is, the more difficult all this becomes. We become used to foibles of our friends and may even find somewhat endearing habits which in strangers we find repelling. Thus is it that churches-in-communion live in practice with a high degree of diversity, while some of these diversities may constitute real barriers to reconciliation between churches once divided.

Moreover, in the course of time new differences develop between separated communities, some of which are in their turn experienced as 'justifying' continued separation. The current debate about *The Gift of Authority* has brought to light difficulties, stereotypes and judgements which owe little or nothing to the religious concerns of the Reformation.

A further example – useful because it may feel more remote – is provided by the non-recognition or non-reception of Chalcedon by the Armenian Apostolic Church. Without tracing the history of this particular theological debate across the centuries, it is worth noting that the stance of the Armenians relates at least in part to their non-participation, for political and military reasons, in the Council.

The position of the Armenians on the Christological questions at stake should not be described as rejection of the

Chalcedonian formulae, nor as a monophysite rejection of the faith they express. Alongside whatever elements there may have been of *amour propre* about a definition made in their absence, there has for long been a feeling in Armenian circles that this was a 'definition too far'. It has been interesting to observe how the discussion about Chalcedon has reopened in recent years between the so-called 'Chalcedonian' and the Oriental Orthodox churches. This illustrates how long the time-lines of reception may be, how contingent factors can obscure mutual recognition and how complicated is the relationship between an essential doctrine and its formulations.

The divisions which ensued endured and to some extent still endure to the present day. To a considerable extent in this as in other examples of schism, it is the division itself which constitutes the biggest single reason for the continuing division. In such circumstances it is necessary to establish some degree of mutual recognition and fellowship as an essential precondition for fuller theological agreement and communion. This is why increasingly shared life is as important as theological dialogue in the ecumenical movement. Indeed, I hope it is clear from what I have already said that shared life is in fact one of the bases of theological dialogue, convergence and consensus.

Reception and the Quest for Unity

None of this is easy! In a Church which inhabits every land and culture and speaks all human languages, it is inevitable that particular churches will develop expressions of the faith which differ from those developed elsewhere and at other times. When the bonds of communion are healthy and in good repair, these characteristics can be moderated by the insight and experience of others and the whole be maintained within the overarching sense of one Church, one faith, one Lord. Otherwise difference and diversity lead to divergence, which is what happens between separated and antagonistic confessions.

The way back to fellowship and mutual recognition and thus to shared re-reception of the one apostolic faith becomes harder and harder. We even encounter the phenomenon of different Christian groups claiming to appeal to Scripture in support of mutually exclusive or contradictory positions, and apparently succeeding in their appeal, to their own satisfaction at least, because they do not realize that they are approaching the Scriptures with hermeneutic tools derived from their own Christian experience which is being lived in a schismatic way.

Nevertheless, even divided Christian lives have to be lived. Decisions have to be taken, moral choices made, the gospel proclaimed. Practically speaking separated churches each have to behave much of the time as if they were the whole Church. We need to be able to be confident in the word preached and the sacraments celebrated, and in our actual participation in the Body of Christ.

On the other hand, there must be limits to this kind of confidence. If Jesus Christ is God's uniquely incarnated Word, we must have some means by which to express our faith and life in him. Hence the importance of distinguishing between those matters which lie at the heart of the faith and those which are less central. This is a crude way of speaking but will do as a working requirement. It is reasonable to suppose that the things closest to the heart of the faith (fundamentals) are the chief matters that Christians should hold in common. These will include those elements that most bind the body together, both within a particular ecclesial family and within the whole Church.

The degree of freedom a particular church or denomination has to develop its own way of doing things should thus depend primarily on the centrality of the issue in question to the fundamentals of the faith. Both in living our own ecclesial life and in evaluating developments in other churches, it is necessary also to take account of the particular pressures which bear on each because of their own cultural environments. We all have a common obligation, which has to be honoured in different ways, to shape our presentation of the common faith and even more so our handling of secondary matters in a way which enables them to give authentic Christian witness in the actual circumstances in which we live. It should be noted that these points apply just as much to churches divided by geography as they do to churches divided by confession.

How Does This Bear on the Episcopal Ministry Act of Synod?

My first conclusion is that we should be cautious about using reception language in the present context unless we are convinced that the ordination of women really is an *articulus stantis vel cadentis ecclesiae*. It could be such for one of two reasons. First, because it is positively enjoined by Scripture and Tradition, or second, because by identifiable criteria of development it can be shown to be the only possible answer to the question once it has been asked.

On the former reason, we would have to give an account of how our synchronic communion is maintained with those in previous ages who had been wrong on such a central matter of faith. On the second reason, we would have to answer a similar question in relation to our synchronic communion now with those who remain in error, whether in our own church or more widely. Ecumenically, it would raise serious questions about many dialogues.

Within the Church of England or the wider Anglican Communion it raises questions about our integrity in maintaining *ad extra* that mutual interchangeability of ministries is an essential ingredient in full visible unity, while we patently do not live that principle in our own life. Indeed our situation is worse than that. Our consistency on the need for interchangeability had already been established for many years before we enshrined limitations to this in the self-same legislation by which we approved the ordination of women to the priesthood. (I am at this point speaking about the Measure itself, not about the Act of Synod.) Thus we find ourselves speaking with a divided voice on what we have maintained is an essential principle, and have even embodied that divided voice in legislation.

And yet this is precisely where we are as a church – indeed it is precisely where the whole Church finds itself. It may not be the first time the Church of England is in the situation of living out in its own body conflicts which in fact belong to the whole Body. The problems are manifold. They concern the nature of holy order and where it stands in relation to the fundamentals of the faith. They concern the nature of gender in the orders of creation and redemption. And of course they concern the issues of reception and communion which have been the subject of this paper.

In the case of holy order and gender we have to ask whether either or both are, to use a common, albeit not very satisfactory distinction, 'first order' or 'second order' questions. If first order, reception is clearly relevant, but must presuppose a certain provisionality about the decision until the whole Church finds a voice. If second order, not only is it questionable whether reception is the proper word to use, but we ought also to conclude with Lutheran and Reformed colleagues that full agreement about the ministry ought not to be required for the unity of the Church. On the other hand, one might reasonably think that to take steps that might divide the Church (undoubtedly a 'first order' question) over a secondary matter would be hard to justify.

The basic issue as it seems to me is that we are not as a church agreed about any of these things. Should we agree to differ, could we agree to differ, and if so for how long? Should we follow the lead of those who wish to harden the lines of our present impaired communion by pressing either for the ordination of women bishops or for a 'third province'? Should we find a way of excluding one or other voice from our fellowship – taking seriously, I hope, what I have said about the relationship between fellowship, recognition and truth?

I do not think we should do any of those things. Given the reality of our situation the main provisions of the legislation and the Act of Synod seem to me to be a good and honest attempt by the Church of England, being the kind of body the Church of England is, to hold together in as high a degree of communion as possible a diversity of views and practice while we ourselves and the wider Church test the nature of the decision we have taken.

The object of 'reception' (taking the legislation as our starting point) thus appears to be not whether women may be priests or not, but whether a church may credibly both admit women to the priesthood and accept conscientious dissent from this development. That must tell us something about how the Church of England understands the nature of ordination. It may not be what we want to hear.

What is ultimately being tested therefore might be thought to be the way in which we make decisions, and the competence of a representative synodical body to adjudicate on fundamental matters of doctrine. If the ordination of women and its relation to the doctrine of holy order are first order questions, are there other first order decisions the Synod might be inhibited from making? Where stands now the traditional Anglican concern to resist innovations for which there is no clear scriptural warrant?

Once again my conclusion is that the Act of Synod may not be what anyone would want, but it provides a framework for shared life at a time at which developments are being sifted but at which precisely which developments are being sifted is by no means easy to discern.

4

THE EPISCOPAL MINISTRY ACT OF SYNOD IN CONTEXT

Mary Tanner

The Episcopal Ministry Act of Synod 1993 can only properly be understood when it is seen in the context of the events and the theological thinking that led up to the passing of the Act in November 1993. This requires rehearsing three separate, yet interrelated stories, which like three Chinese boxes fit one inside of the other. The reason why it is necessary to engage with three stories and not just with one is because of the way in which Anglicans understand their identity and unity.

At the Reformation the English Church rejected the jurisdiction of the Bishop of Rome, but understood itself as the continuing catholic Church in this land. Unlike the German Reformers, the ministry of the Church of England did not represent a radical or deliberate break with the threefold ministry of the Western Church. Anglicans make no claim to being the whole Church but understand themselves as part of the one, holy, catholic and apostolic Church, professing the apostolic faith, celebrating the sacraments, and continuing the ministry in the historic episcopal succession, of the Church through the ages. This understanding of Anglican identity is fundamental in the consideration of the ordination of women to the priesthood and the Episcopal Ministry Act of Synod. It is the reason why the Church of England story has to be considered within both the ecumenical and Anglican Communion stories.

The Ecumenical Story

The majority of Christendom, namely, the Roman Catholic, the Eastern Orthodox and the Oriental Orthodox Churches, do not ordain women. They hold that they have not the authority to change the tradition of an all-male priesthood. Popes and cardinals have exchanged letters with Archbishops of Canterbury making the position clear. The official Vatican line has hardened over recent years, in spite of, perhaps because of, movements in favour of the ordination of women among its own people. The Orthodox churches too have continued to show their disapproval over developments within the Anglican Communion. On the other hand, many of the churches of the Reformation have ordained women to the presbyterate and women now are in oversight roles in those churches. Two churches of the Porvoo communion (the relationship of communion between Nordic and Baltic Lutheran churches and the Anglican churches of Britain and Ireland) have women bishops. The theological debates, as well as the practical experience, of both churches that do and those that do not ordain women, is an essential context for understanding the Church of England's response to the movement towards women's ordination in general and the Act of Synod in particular.

The Anglican Communion's Story

Since 1960, when Hong Kong first raised the issue of women's ordination, the matter has never been seen as a matter for an individual province to decide. Hong Kong did not claim the right to act unilaterally but first referred the matter to the Lambeth Conference in 1968. That Conference asked each province to study the question and to report back to the newly established Anglican Consultative Council (ACC). The ACC met for the first time two years later in 1970 in Limuru. The consultative process on women's ordination was unfinished. Indeed it had hardly begun. Nevertheless, the Council advised the Bishop of Hong Kong that should his own Synod decided to ordain women this action would be acceptable to the ACC. The Council would use its own good offices to encourage all provinces to remain 'in communion' with him and his church. The understanding of the notion of communion (*koinonia*) has been central to the discussion ever since. The next Lambeth Conference in 1978 did not make a definitive judgement for the whole Communion on the validity, or otherwise, of ordinations of women. The bishops agreed to respect the positions of both those who favoured women's ordination and those who did not. Resolution 21 declared its acceptance of member churches that do ordain, urging respect for those provinces, and *vice versa*. This Resolution led to some confusion. Some bishops left the 1978 Lambeth Conference believing that the validity of such ordinations had been settled, others were equally convinced that it had not been settled.

By Lambeth 1988 the question had moved from the issue of women priests to the consideration of women as bishops. In 1985 the Episcopal Church of the United States of America (ECUSA) had expressed the intention not to withhold consent to the election of a bishop on the grounds of gender. However, sensitive to the interdependence of the provinces of the Anglican Communion, ECUSA referred the matter to the newly created Primates' Meeting. The Primates set up a working party under the chairmanship of Archbishop Grindrod of Australia to prepare for a discussion of the matter at the 1988 Lambeth Conference. It was the thinking of the Grindrod Working Party that was to become determinative, not only for the decision taken at the 1988 Lambeth Conference on women and the episcopate, but also for much of the thinking that subsequently conditioned the debates, within both the Anglican Communion and the Church of England, including the discussions that led up to the Episcopal Ministry Act of Synod.[1]

The Grindrod Report teased out both the theological and the practical issues involved in the debate on the consecration of women as bishops. It set before the college of bishops at the Lambeth Conference two possible options in respect of the consecration of women as bishops. The first option was to counsel restraint in the hope that the moral authority inherent in the gathering of the entire episcopate would find its response in restraint at the provincial level. The second option was to suggest that, if a province were persuaded by compelling doctrinal reasons, by the experience of women in ordained ministry, by the demands of mission in its region, and if it had the overwhelming support of its dioceses, then such a step to consecrate a woman should be offered for reception both in the Anglican Communion and in the universal Church. From this point on the notion of reception became fundamental in understanding actions taken by provinces in respect of women's ordination.

In the event the bishops at the 1988 Lambeth Conference resolved:

1. That each Province respect the decision and attitude of other Provinces in the ordination (or consecration) of women to the episcopate, without such respect necessarily indicating acceptance of the principles involved, maintaining the highest degree of communion with the Provinces which differ.[2]

Once again the Lambeth Conference of 1988 made no attempt to state whether it was, or was not, right to ordain women. It did, however, lay great stress on the qualities required of both sides, tolerance, respect and the wish to

[1] *Women and the Episcopate: The Grindrod Report* (Anglican Consultative Council, 1988).

[2] *The Truth Shall Make You Free*, The Lambeth Conference 1988 (London: Church House Publishing, 1988).

maintain the highest degree of communion possible, resolving:

> 2. That bishops exercise courtesy and maintain communications with bishops who may differ, and with any woman bishop, ensuring an open dialogue in the Church to whatever extent communion is impaired.

The resolution went on to call on the Archbishop of Canterbury, in consultation with the Primates, to appoint a commission:

> 3. (a) to provide for an examination of the relationships between Provinces of the Anglican Communion and ensure that the process of reception includes continuing consultation with other churches as well;
> (b) to monitor and encourage the process of consultation within the Communion and to offer further pastoral guidelines.

A Commission, under the chairmanship of Archbishop Robin Eames of Armagh, went on to produce five reports.[3] These reports contain factual information about what was happening in the Communion, theological reflection, and pastoral guidelines for how to live together in the 'highest degree of communion' where there exists a diversity of opinion. It was clear to the Eames Commission that two distinct views continued to be held in the Anglican Communion. The notion of 'reception', crucial in the thinking of *The Grindrod Report,* became more and more important in interpreting what was going on in the Anglican Communion. If a province were to proceed to ordain women, that development in the ordering of the universal ministry was understood as being given up to a process of discernment in the province concerned, in all the provinces of the Anglican Communion, and further as being offered to the universal Church for wider discernment. The matter of women's

---

[3] *Women in the Anglican Episcopate, Theology, Guidelines and Practice*, The Eames Commission and the Monitoring Group Reports (Toronto: Anglican Book Centre, 1998).

ordination could not be declared to be settled, beyond any shadow of doubt, until it was received by the whole Church. Anglicans on both sides were urged to go on respecting each other's deeply held convictions, respecting the integrity of one another, in an open process of discernment, and remaining in the highest degree of communion possible. Such a process was described as a 'process of open reception'.

It was this understanding of a dynamic, ongoing process of 'open reception' that in part led the college of bishops in ECUSA to put forward a scheme of episcopal visitors to care for those who, being opposed to women priests, were fearful that the efficacy of the sacraments would be endangered by a change in the gender of the person ordained, as well as by those ordained by her. It is important to underline that it was the development in the ordering of the ministry which was the question at issue and not the validity of the priesthood or the episcopate of any woman legally ordained in a province that went forward on this matter.

For the Eames Commission, with its understanding of the Anglican Communion as part of the Catholic Church, together with its understanding of the process of discernment and reception, it was crucial that those in favour of women's ordination should go on showing why it is gospel truth that women should be ordained and that those against should go on showing why it is contrary to the gospel message. There were to be no alternative conciliar structures, no separate province established for those with opposing views. This could only lead to two groups defining themselves over against each other with separate badges of identity based on attitudes to women's ordination. If the reception process were indeed to be 'open' then both sides needed each other within a single conciliar and synodal life. This would entail the costly way of listening to the other and struggling to understand the position of the other – respecting the integrity of the other. In the space between testifying and listening, listening and testifying, room is made for the Holy Spirit to guide the Church into all truth. Thus, the process of reception was seen as a 'spiritual process'.

The Church of England Story

The two stories traced so far are integral to, and inseparable from, the third story, the move to ordain women in the Church of England and the Episcopal Ministry Act of Synod that followed.

Many reports and debates in the Church of England led up to a synodical resolution in 1975 that 'there are no fundamental objections to the ordination of women to the priesthood', a statement which may be thought to look very different today in the light of subsequent events. In 1984 the General Synod passed the 'Southwark motion' which asked the Synod to bring forward legislation to permit the ordination of women to the priesthood. There was confusion and horror in 1986 in response to *The McClean Report* (GS 738) that outlined safeguards for bishops and parishes unable to accept women priests, financial provisions to relieve the hardship of those who felt obliged to resign, and five possible options for providing for those who wished to remain in the Church of England while unable to accept the ministrations of a bishop who ordained women. Those options ranged from the delegation of episcopal ministry to a bishop designated by the archbishop of the province to the complete separation of resources into two separate churches. The fear of this latter stark suggestion terrified many and had a profound effect on the legislation that eventually appeared. It was at this point that the bishops flexed their collegial muscles and persuaded the General Synod to postpone further consideration of the ordination of women until they themselves, as a House, were able to report to the Synod.

In February 1987 the House of Bishops published *The*

Ordination of Women to the Priesthood (GS 764). Part I set out the theological issues about which the Synod would have to satisfy itself if it were to move to ordain women. Reflections on the role of a bishop and the role of collegiality in maintaining the unity of the Church, the 'glue' that binds the Church together, as well as the reflections on decision-making when Christendom is divided, were formative in everything that followed. Picking up the work of the Eames Commission the Church of England bishops stressed that, if the Synod went ahead to approve women's ordination, its decision would necessarily be put to a process of reception, of open reception.

> A measure of continuing discussion would be appropriate within a province, between provinces, and between Churches in the ecumenical movement. It might be possible for those who remain opposed to the ordination of women to remain within the communion of a Church that ordains women, providing that all understand that practice within the perspective of a continuing open process of reception.[4]

The bishops set out principles that should underlie legislation. It is interesting to recall what some of these were and to reflect on how far they were, or were not, in fact, followed. The bishops said:

- There ought to be room in the Church for those who remained for the time being agnostic and who were unwilling to accept the ministrations of women. However, for some groups not to recognise lawfully ordained ministers would inevitably threaten the inner communion of the Church of England. (para. 29)
- If the Church of England were to decide to ordain women, those who continued within it and who remained opposed to this decision would need at the very least to respect the Church's order and decision and

---

[4] *The Ordination of Women to the Priesthood: A Report by the House of Bishops*, GS 764 (London: Church House, 1987), para. 26.

to act within the safeguards provided. (The same would be true if the decision were to go the other way.) In both cases actively to seek to frustrate the Church's order and decisions would be to act against the ministry of the Church which is the bond of the communion of the Church ... those remaining opposed might seek to reverse the decision through legitimate means as part of the process of reception by the wider Church. (para. 30)

- It is difficult to see how a PCC, or a parish priest, could refuse the ministrations of a diocesan bishop without straining the communion and order of the Church ... There is no theological justification for the view that the subsequent sacramental actions undertaken by bishops who had ordained women to the priesthood are thereby invalidated. (para. 35)

- Because of the relation of the bishop to his diocese it would destroy that relationship if a diocesan bishop, unwilling to ordain women to the priesthood, were to delegate that function to a suffragan or area bishop. For once there is a woman priest within a diocese, the bishop of the diocese has a role in relation to her as to any male priest within his jurisdiction. ... To deny the validity of her priesthood by refusing to participate in her ordination would break the communion between bishop and presbyters and prevent full collegial life within that diocese. (para. 37)

- Once a province has expressed its mind in favour of the ordination of women to the priesthood and proceeded so to ordain women it would be anomalous to appoint a bishop who was actively opposed to the mind of the province, and in particular opposed to the common mind of the college of bishops. (para. 40)

Reading this after some years it can be seen that the bishops and the Church of England were struggling to find the way ahead. Looking back we can also see that not all of the things the bishops said in their report here were eventually accepted or acted upon.

In addition to reflections on the principles behind legislation, the bishops offered a framework for legislation and safeguards – safeguards for parishes, priests, and bishops in office if and when women were ordained, as well as a measure of financial provision for those who felt they must leave.

It was this Bishops' Report (GS 764) which provided the basis for the final legislation that was accepted in November 1992. It is worth noting three things in relation to the passing of the legislation.

First, the voting figures: in the diocesan synod voting, 38 out of the 44 diocesan synods approved the motions to ordain women; in the deanery synods 62.5 per cent of clergy and 66.1 per cent of laity supported the legislation; and in the General Synod there was a 75 per cent majority in favour in the House of Bishops, a 70.4 per cent majority in the House of Clergy, and a 67.3 per cent majority in the House of Laity. These figures suggest that there remained a sizeable minority opposed.

Second, at the revision stage of the legislation, the 20-year time limit imposed on safeguards was deleted. The Archbishop of York's advice to the General Synod was that opponents of women's ordination saw the 20-year time limit as a threat and, therefore, it should be rejected. A time limit he suggested was in fact contrary to the theory of 'open reception'.

Third, the debate on the legislation in 1988 was preceded by a debate on the theological issues, based upon a substantial theological report by the House: *The Ordination of Women to the Priesthood: A Second Report by the House of Bishops* (GS 829). This report examined the issues involved showing the range of opinions that existed within the House on each issue. This might be thought to be tantamount to calling into question the 1975 decision that there were no 'fundamental objections' to the ordination of women.

Almost immediately after the vote in favour of women's ordination in November 1992 attention focused on those who remained opposed – a sizeable minority. Two Measures had to go to Parliament for approval, through the Ecclesiastical Committee, before women could be ordained. The parliamentary process provided an interval for further reflection by the House of Bishops on how the Church of England might live with difference on the matter of women's ordination. In January 1993 the bishops met in Manchester and unanimously agreed a way forward which they set out in *The Manchester Statement*. Stories have been told of that meeting, of fears that were expressed and the joyful bursting into song when the Statement was approved. The concerns of those opposed and the pressure from the Ecclesiastical Committee of Parliament led the bishops to suggest that the Manchester proposals should be embodied in an Act of Synod, which, though not legally binding, would have a 'moral' force and could only be revoked by the General Synod itself.

The Manchester Statement acknowledged that the majority of bishops welcomed the Synod's decision to ordain women and that the bishops looked forward to the new gifts women would bring to ordained ministry. It was, however, to those opposed that the bishops wished to give 'every reassurance'. They stressed that the November 1992 decision had to be seen in the context of a wider process of reception, in the Church of England, the Anglican Communion and the universal Church. Those opposed were valued and loyal members of the Anglican family. 'Differing views can continue to be held with integrity' (para. 4). 'All must listen with respect to those from whom they differ and afford a recognition of the value and integrity of each other's position' (para. 5). 'It is no shame to agree both to differ and to live, sometimes fearfully, together in the service of God.'[5]

Finally, the bishops said that in accommodating a diversity of convictions:

> We are committed to maintaining the overall unity of the Church, including the unity of each diocese under the jurisdiction of the diocesan bishop. We believe such unity is essential to the overall effectiveness of the Church's mission to bring the Gospel of Christ to all people. (para. 8)

> We intend to ensure that provision continues to be made by the diocesan bishop for the care and oversight of everyone in his diocese. (para. 9)

The bishops quoted Resolution 72 of the 1988 Lambeth Conference on 'episcopal responsibilities and diocesan boundaries'. That resolution had reaffirmed 'its unity in the historical position of respect for diocesan boundaries and the authority of bishops within these boundaries'. They also affirmed 'that it is deemed as inappropriate behaviour for any bishop or priest of this Communion to exercise episcopal or pastoral ministry within another diocese without first obtaining the permission and invitation of the ecclesial authority thereof'.[6]

Each diocesan bishop in the Church of England would continue to accept full responsibility for episcopal oversight and pastoral care in his diocese. 'Wherever necessary he will extend this care in appropriate ways' (para. 10).

> In making such provision we do not and we cannot accept the theological reasoning behind the view that in some way those bishops and priests who participate in the ordination of women to the priesthood, therefore invalidate their sacramental ministry. Further, we envisage that any bishop appointed to assist us in making any extended sacramental provision, will remain in full communion with all members of the House of Bishops irre-

---

[5] *The Manchester Statement*, January 1993.
[6] *The Truth Shall Make You Free*, p. 240.

spective of whether or not such members have ordained women priests. (para. 11)

It is important to note that what was being suggested was extended episcopal care.

The draft Episcopal Ministry Act of Synod was published five months later in the Bishops' Report, *Bonds of Peace* (GS 1074), with an accompanying theological paper, *Being in Communion* (GS Misc. 480). The bishops explained again that their proposals were designed to hold those of differing views within the Church of England, to recognize both positions and to provide 'space' in which sensible and practical arrangements could be made for those of differing views, without jeopardizing the ecclesiological integrity of the Church. Both those in favour and those opposed were seen to hold legitimate positions while the universal Church comes to a common mind. The bishops talked of 'maintaining the integrity of both positions', a phrasing that was sharply attacked by the Bishop of Durham and others. The Church of England he argued could not hold two integrities. It could, and should, recognize the integrity of those who hold different positions. This in fact echoed the more nuanced language of the earlier *Manchester Statement*.

The report talked of a communion in dialogue, continuing together in discerning truth. The bishops pleaded for courtesy, tolerance, mutual respect, prayer for one another and a desire to know one another and be with one another. The danger that where 'ecclesial communion is impaired', communities will define themselves over against each other and develop apart from, and in isolation from, one another must be avoided. Another danger to be avoided was that where ecclesial communion is impaired through a lack of full interchangeability of ministries, communities would come to define themselves over against one another solely by their position in regard to the single issue of women's ordination. For this reason there was to be no marginalizing of the other, no marginalizing of self, no withdrawal from the councils and government of the Church of England or of the Anglican Communion. In fact conciliarity was seen to be even more important for maintaining the life of communion.

The House went on to suggest how dioceses and parishes might live with diversity, with generosity:

> It will be a sign of continuing communion of bishops and a mark of collegiality when a diocesan bishop, who does not himself accept the ordination of women to the priesthood, but does not make any of the declarations in Clause 2 of the Measure, thereby does not prevent a woman being ordained and licensed by another bishop to minister as priest in his diocese. Similarly, it will be a mark of continuing communion when a diocesan bishop in favour invites a bishop who does not accept it to minister to priests and congregations in his diocese who do themselves not accept it. In both cases oversight remains ultimately with the diocesan bishop, who remains the focus of unity in his diocese, even when he chooses to extend his oversight through another bishop. Such extension should be seen as an expression of the collegiality of the House of Bishops, which accepts the legitimacy of both positions. (para. 5)

The prize of this statement was that when women were ordained no bishop in office availed himself of Clause 2 of the Measure, and no diocese became a 'no-go' area. This was important for those who viewed developments within a process of 'open reception'.

This was the context in which the Episcopal Ministry Act of Synod was framed. The focus now was on the question of how those who were opposed should be cared for? First, each diocesan bishop, as ordinary, was responsible for the care and oversight of everyone in his diocese and, wherever possible, he would make arrangements within his diocese. Second, if this were not possible, he would seek to extend his episcopal care by inviting a bishop from outside his diocese who was opposed to share his care. The effective way would be to implement regional solutions. Bishops meeting regionally would nominate bishops in their region who were suitable. Such bishops would be approved by the archbishop of the province to carry out episcopal duties on behalf of a diocesan. However, the oath of allegiance of all clergy would still be made to the diocesan. Diocesan and regional arrangements for episcopal care were to be prior. However, 'to supplement the diocesan and regional arrangements, the Archbishop of Canterbury proposed to appoint up to two additional suffragans for his dioceses and the Archbishop of York one suffragan bishop for his dioceses, to undertake duties across the province on a similar basis to the bishops appointed to act regionally'. These Provincial Episcopal Visitors would be nominated by the archbishops after consultation with those bishops directly concerned with the Visitors Ministry.

The Provincial Episcopal Visitors were to work with the diocesan bishop concerned in enabling extended pastoral care and sacramental ministry. They were also to act as spokesmen and advisors for those who were opposed to women's ordination and to assist the archbishops in maintaining the arrangements made for them.

The Episcopal Ministry Act of Synod was not only about Provincial Episcopal Visitors. It was concerned to provide episcopal care for those who were opposed to women's ordination, first by internal diocesan arrangements. If this proved impossible then regional arrangements were to be put in place. Only to supplement that system were Provincial Episcopal Visitors to be considered.

The Episcopal Ministry Act of Synod was approved on 11 November 1993 by an extraordinarily high majority of the General Synod (39–0 Bishops; 175–12 Clergy; 194–4 Laity). Synodical approval was also given to up to three new suffragan sees for Provincial Episcopal Visitors, two in the province of Canterbury and one in the province of York.

This is the Church of England story, a story within two other stories – the Anglican Communion story and the ecumenical story. No-one could accuse the Church of England either of taking its decision lightly, or of acting as an autonomous province without any regard for the interdependence of the provinces of the Communion. Nor could it be said that the Church of England was not mindful of the wider ecumenical scene. Nor could it be said that the bishops neglected their role in guiding the Church. The college of bishops played an increasingly active role in guiding the Church, not being afraid to make public its reflections, which showed the way its thinking was developing and even, in some cases, the way it was being modified.

The Act of Synod was the end of a long process in which theological and ecclesiological concepts shaped what happened. First, there was a growing acceptance, contrary to the 1975 motion that 'there are no fundamental objections', that different opinions on the matter did exist and could be held with integrity. Second, there was an increasing awareness that decisions about the universal ministry, taken in a divided Christendom, necessarily have a degree of provisionality about them. Provisionality must not be taken as referring to the ministry of any individual woman, but rather to the development of women's ordination within the ordering of the ministry itself. Third, the move to ordain women must, therefore, be given over to an open process of reception within the Anglican Communion and the universal Church. Discernment and reception are vital. Fourth, the understanding of the Church as communion became the fundamental ecclesiological concept in understanding the nature of the Church and its mission. It also provided a vital clue to interpreting what was happening. Fifth, the understanding of episcopal ministry as 'the glue' that holds the Church in communion and, therefore, the need to maintain collegiality and the highest degree of interchangeability of ministry was crucial. The bishop, as sign and focus of unity, the one who exercises jurisdiction and remains the ordinary, was important for developing the role of the Provincial Episcopal Visitor's ministry and for understanding the place and character of extended episcopal oversight. And, finally, it was crucial to the Act of Synod that the gospel values that St Paul wrote about in his day – courtesy and respect, tolerance and patience, sticking with the other – were to determine the quality of life together in the Church of England.

It has not been my job here to pass judgement on the Episcopal Ministry Act of Synod, one way or another, but simply to tell this fascinating story. What the bishops said remains crucial:

> Our attempt to do this (that is to live with difference) has significance not only for ourselves but also for the wider church and for a world, which desperately needs to learn that art of living together with difference.

5

COMMUNION AND THE KINGDOM OF GOD

Robert Hannaford

Introduction

The decision by the General Synod of the Church of England in 1992 to legislate for the ordination of women to the priesthood while many within the Church remained opposed created a serious pastoral situation. Opponents believed, and continue to believe, that the ordination of women to the priesthood is inconsistent with the historic tradition of the Church. The challenge facing the Church of England was to create the conditions in which opponents could in conscience remain within the Church. To many Christians, inside and outside the Church of England, a difference of opinion about the ordained ministry might seem secondary and peripheral. However, matters of order are not so lightly dismissed. They touch upon the sacramental and representational life of the Church. A church where some members hold the orders of those duly and canonically ordained in doubt is a church that is visibly divided. This state of affairs is obviously very serious indeed and constitutes a long-term challenge for the Church of England. Our concern in this chapter is with the church's more immediate response to the pastoral needs of those who could not accept women's ordination to the priesthood.

The challenge created by the legislation was twofold. First, to secure a space for the legitimate expression of dissent and, second, to create conditions for the maintenance of the highest degree of communion between those with

opposing views. The situation was put very succinctly in the
House of Bishops Working Party Report *Being in Communion*, which was published shortly after the 1992 vote:

> We now enter a process in which it is desirable that both those in
> favour and those opposed should be recognised as holding
> legitimate positions while the whole Church seeks to come to a
> common mind. The Church of England needs to understand itself
> as a communion in dialogue, committed to remaining together in
> the ongoing process of the discernment of truth within the wider
> fellowship of the Christian Church. Giving space to each other,
> and remaining in the highest possible degree of communion in
> spite of differences are crucial, as we strive to be open to the
> insights of the wider Christian community.[1]

The foundations upon which the Church was to develop its
strategy for responding to the twin challenges are laid out
in this report. Opponents of women's ordination to the
priesthood were not merely to be tolerated but recognized
as holding a 'legitimate' position. As the report continues,
'The bishops, corporately and individually, are pledged to
maintain the integrity of both positions.'[2] This was regarded as a prerequisite for creating the conditions necessary
for the 'ongoing process of the discernment of truth'. Those
who cannot accept the ordination of women to the priesthood were encouraged to participate fully in the life of the
Church, 'except in those matters where conscientious convictions are directly at stake'.[3] In making this proviso the
compilers of the report undoubtedly had in mind the view
of many opponents that the ordination of women priests
would affect the communion of clergy and congregations
with their bishop. The report commends a pastoral policy
whereby a diocesan bishop in favour of the ordination of
women to the priesthood would invite a bishop who does
not accept it to 'minister to priests and congregations in his

[1] *Being in Communion*, GS Misc. 418 (London: Church House, 1993), pp. 18f.
[2] *Being in Communion*, p. 19.
[3] *Being in Communion*.

diocese who themselves do not accept it'.[4] Significantly this is described as a 'mark of continuing communion'.[5] It was important that exceptional provisions should be seen as promoting communion, even when they were at another level signalling its impairment.

It may seem puzzling to some readers that the debate following the decision to ordain women to the priesthood should resolve upon the question of bishops. Some explanation is called for. Within the threefold order of bishops, priests and deacons Anglican polity accords a distinctive role to the episcopate. Not all Anglicans would accept the explication of this by Dom Gregory Dix, but it represents the position of many, not least among those opposed to the ordination of women to the priesthood:

> The ... bishop is ... in a singular sense 'the man' of his own Church – its priest, offering its corporate sacrifice by which it 'becomes what it is', the Body of Christ, which is at once the climax and source of its being as a Church; and the minister, in person or by delegation, of all sacraments to all its members. He is also, by his liturgical sermon, the guardian and spokesman to itself and to the world without of his own Church's doctrinal tradition, by which the apostolic function of 'witness to revelation' is discharged. He is the creator of its lesser ministers; its representative to other Churches; the administrator of its charity; the officer of its discipline; the centre of its unity; the hub of its whole many-sided life, spiritual, temporal, inward and outward.[6]

The rite for the Ordination or Consecration of a Bishop in the Ordinal of *The Alternative Service Book* states that the bishop 'as a chief pastor ... shares with his fellow bishops a special responsibility to maintain and further the unity of the Church'.[7] It is not in the character of Anglicanism to

[4] Ibid.
[5] Ibid.
[6] Dom G. Dix, 'Ministry in the Early Church', in K.E. Kirk (ed.), *The Apostolic Ministry* (London: Hodder and Stoughton, 1946), pp. 198f.
[7] 'The Ordination or Consecration of a Bishop', in *The Alternative Service Book 1980*, p. 388.

spell out the theological implications of this 'special responsibility' in precise detail in its historic formularies. Nonetheless, the Church of England's canon law makes it clear that the bishop has ordinary jurisdiction within his diocese. All who minister in his diocese do so under his authority and in effect share in his ministry. The bishop has the primary responsibility within the local church (i.e. the diocese) for its visible communion in word and sacrament. The 1990 Report of the Archbishops' Group on the Episcopate did not hesitate to express this in the strongest possible terms:

> In the local church the bishop focuses and nurtures the unity of his people; in his sharing in the collegiality of bishops the local church is bound together with the other local churches; and through the succession of bishops the local community is related to the Church through the ages. Thus the bishop in his own person in his diocese; and in his collegial relations in the wider church; and through his place in the succession of bishops in their communities in faithfulness to the Gospel, is a sign and focus of the unity of the Church.[8]

Priests and deacons exercise their own distinctive ministries but always in communion with their diocesan bishop. The licence given to each parish priest makes it clear that his or her ministry is shared with the bishop, and since the earliest days of the Church deacons have had a particularly close association with the bishop. The primacy of the bishop means that he is the principal celebrant of the sacrament of orders. Priests are ordained to share in the bishop's ministry as principal celebrant of the Eucharist within the local church. Deacons for their part are ordained to share in the bishop's ministry as ambassador and bridge-builder. As a recent report puts it: 'The special role of deacons is to make connections and build bridges between the distinctive life,

---

[8] *Episcopal Ministry: The Report of the Archbishops' Group on the Episcopate* (London: Church House Publishing, 1990), p. 160.

the *koinonia*, of the Body of Christ and the needs of the world.'[9]

As a 'focus of unity' in the diocese the bishop is a 'sign of assurance to the faithful that the Church remains in continuity with the apostles' teaching and mission'.[10] The ministry of deacons and priests within the diocese is therefore intimately related to that of the bishop. First, in the sense that each deacon and priest acts for and hence represents his or her bishop. Second, in the sense that the ministry of leadership and pastoral care is most fully embodied in the episcopal office. The ministry of deacons and priests is, as it were, a sacramental derivation of the ministry of the bishop. It follows from this that the bishop is implicated in the ministry of all of his clergy and *vice versa*. What the bishop does – and, to a lesser extent this is true also of those who minister under his authority – touches upon the unity and life of the whole diocese.

It is clear then that for Anglicans each priest and deacon represents and participates in the ministry of the bishop. This helps to explain why *Being in Communion* made the suggestion that a bishop in favour of the ordination of women to the priesthood might extend his 'oversight through another bishop' who does not.[11] The bishops had earlier distanced themselves from the view that bishops and priests who participate in the ordination of women to the priesthood thereby invalidate their sacramental ministry.[12] Nonetheless they recognized that such ordinations would place a strain upon the communion of some clergy and

[9] *For Such a Time as This: A Renewed Diaconate in the Church of England*. A report to the General Synod of the Church of England of a Working Party of the House of Bishops (London: Church House Publishing, 2001), p. 52.

[10] *Apostolicity and Succession*. House of Bishops Occasional Paper, GS Misc. 432 (London: Church House Publishing, 1994), para. 60.

[11] *Being in Communion*, p. 19.

[12] Statement by the House of Bishops following its meeting in Manchester, 11–14 January 1993, para. 11.

congregations with their bishop. Many who oppose the ordination of women to the priesthood do so because they see it as a threat to the visible continuity of the Church's communion in the faith. The presence of women in his college of priests would call into question for them the bishop's role as the ministerial embodiment of the local church's faithfulness to the historic faith. Ordaining women to the priesthood was not seen as the only signal of discontinuity. The continuing ministry of women priests, who in the nature of things would be acting in the name of their diocesan bishop, would reinforce it.

The Episcopal Ministry Act of Synod 1993

In responding to the difficulties outlined above the House of Bishops brought before the General Synod an Act which they believed would address many of the hesitations felt by opponents to the ordination of women priests. The Act enshrined many of the principles already outlined in *Being in Communion*. It affirmed the equal integrity of both positions on the question at issue. It also stated that all concerned should endeavour to ensure that 'the highest possible degree of communion should be maintained within each diocese.' More controversially, it sought to put into practice practical pastoral arrangements to address the question of episcopal communion. This was to be achieved by building upon the principle of 'extended episcopal care'.

The arrangements were aimed at ensuring 'appropriate care and oversight' of clergy and parishes. Parochial church councils could petition their diocesan bishop, to appoint a bishop opposed to the ordination of women to the priesthood, to carry out appropriate episcopal duties in that parish. The Act of Synod envisaged three types of arrangements: diocesan, regional and provincial. In the case of the first two diocesan bishops would draw upon the services of other full-time stipendiary bishops opposed to the ordination of women to the priesthood in their dioceses or regions. In the case of the third the archbishops would appoint additional suffragan bishops within their dioceses to act as 'provincial episcopal visitors'. In fact three such suffragan sees have been created: two in the province of Canterbury and one in the province of York. In addition to the normal duties of suffragan bishops, the Act specifies two basic roles for the episcopal visitors, or 'flying bishops', as they have come to be known. First, to work with the diocesan bishop in 'enabling extended pastoral care and sacramental ministry to be provided'. Second, to act as spokesmen and advisors for those opposed to the ordination of women to the priesthood.

In his introduction to *Bonds of Peace*, a report issued by the House of Bishops, the Archbishop of Canterbury commended the above arrangements on the grounds that they:

> are designed to hold within the Church of England those of differing views on the ordination of women to the priesthood. They seek to recognise the position both of those in favour and those against, and to provide space in which sensible practical arrangements for those of differing views can be made without jeopardising the ecclesiological integrity of the Church.[13]

In taking up principles already outlined in *Being in Communion* four things are clear from these words:

> First, that the Act is a pastoral provision designed to serve the *koinonia* of the Church.

> Second, that the Act is intended to create a space for reflection and debate on the ordination of women to the priesthood.

> Third, that the Act presupposes the integrity of those who oppose the ordination of women to the priesthood as well as those who support it.

[13] *Ordination of Women to the Priesthood: Pastoral Arrangements*, A Report by the House of Bishops, GS Misc. 1074 (London: General Synod, 1993), p. 2f.

Finally, that its provisions are seen as consistent with the ecclesiological integrity of the Church of England.

Each of these points is important but we shall concentrate on the first and the fourth. The debate about the Act usually focuses on the narrower question of the theology of orders, particularly the role of the episcopate. In what follows I would like to offer an assessment of the Act's pastoral provisions in the light of the *koinonia* of the whole Church.

Following the Lambeth conference of Anglican bishops in 1988, the Archbishop of Canterbury established an international commission on women and the episcopate, chaired by Archbishop Robin Eames. In its first report the commission defended the provision of episcopal visitors, which had first been mooted in a resolution of the 1988 General Convention of the Episcopal Church of the USA, as 'a necessary and strictly extraordinary anomaly in preference to schism'.[14] Notwithstanding difficulties at the level of the theology of holy order, our argument will be that the Act of Synod, and specifically the creation of episcopal visitors, is a legitimate and creative expression of the discipleship of *koinonia*.

The Ecclesiology of Communion

J.M.R. Tillard has described *koinonia* (generally translated as 'communion', 'fellowship' or 'participation' in English translations of the New Testament) as the basis of the ancient patristic vision of the Church.[15] Cyprian, for example, described the Church as the 'sacrament of unity'. We do not have the space to examine Tillard's claim in

---

[14] 'The First Report', *The Eames Commission: The Official Reports* (Toronto: Anglican Book Centre, 1994), para. 55. Excerpted from *The Eames Commission: The Official Reports*. Copyright 1994 The Secretary General of the Anglican Consultative Council. Used by permission.

[15] J.M.R. Tillard, *Church of Churches: The Ecclesiology of Communion* (Collegeville, Minnesota: Liturgical Press, 1992).

detail, but it should be noted that one would look in vain for a systematic treatment of communion ecclesiology in patristic thought. This is hardly surprising. Ecclesiology (the doctrine of the Church) only emerged as a distinct area of theological enquiry in the modern age, and particularly as a consequence of divisions created in the Western Church at the Reformation.[16]

In a recent study Dennis M. Doyle locates the origins of modern communion ecclesiology in the work of two nineteenth-century theologians: the Catholic theologian Johann Adam Möhler and the Protestant theologian Friedrich Schleiermacher.[17] Although neither used the expression 'communion ecclesiology', they laid foundations that would be taken up by twentieth-century theologians such as Yves Congar and Henri de Lubac. By the 1960s this approach to the doctrine of the Church was well established, to the extent that it emerged as 'the horizontal line around which the major ecclesiological affirmations of the Second Vatican Council revolve'.[18] Theologians of all traditions[19] have taken it up since then, and many would agree with Pope John Paul II, that 'Communion is the very mystery of the

---

[16] See the discussion of the emergence of ecclesiology as a separate area of theological research in G.H. Tavard, *The Church, Community of Salvation: An Ecumenical Ecclesiology*, Collegeville Minnesota: The Liturgical Press, 1992, pp. 7–13; Pannenberg, W., *Systematic Theology*, 3 vols (Edinburgh: T & T Clark, 1998), vol. 3, pp. 21–7, and the helpful brief summary in G. Rowell's 'Editorial: Newman and Ecclesiology', *International Journal for the Study of the Christian Church* 1 (2001): 1–8, esp. pp. 1ff.

[17] D.M. Doyle, *Communion Ecclesiology: Vision and Versions* (Maryknoll New York: Orbis Books, 2000), pp. 23–37.

[18] Tillard, *Church of Churches*, p. xi. See also J. Ratzinger, 'The Ecclesiology of the Second Vatican Council', *Communio* 13 (1986): 239–52.

[19] See, for example, P. Avis, *Christians in Communion* (London: Geoffrey Chapman Mowbray, 1990), Anglican; M. Volf, *After Our Likeness: The Church as the Image of the Trinity*, (Grand Rapids Michigan: Eerdmans, 1998), Baptist; J. Zizioulas, *Being as Communion: Studies in Personhood and the Church* (Crestwood, New York: St Vladimir's Press, 1985), Orthodox.

Church'.[20] We will take this development as the backdrop to our enquiry.

A number of scholars have pointed out that *koinonia* is only a middle-level term in the New Testament, occurring a total of nineteen times, and that it is nowhere treated as synonymous with the term 'Church'.[21] That having been said, Paul certainly uses it in contexts that bear very directly on the life of the Church. So, for example in 1 Corinthians 10.6 we read:

> The cup of blessing which we bless, is it not a participation (*koinonia*) in the blood of Christ? The bread which we break, is it not a participation (*koinonia*) in the body of Christ?

The context – a discussion about the eating of food sacrificed to idols – makes it clear that Paul is establishing a parallel between the body of Jesus sacrificed on the cross and the Christian community as the 'body of Christ'. The passage unites Christology and ecclesiology by means of the stress on Christian fellowship or participation in the sacramental life of Christ: 'because there is one bread, we who are many are one body, for we all partake of the one bread' (1 Corinthians 10.17). The eucharistic associations of *koinonia* also serve to highlight the eschatological dimensions of the concept. Those who participate in the eucharistic meal 'proclaim the Lord's death until he comes' (1 Corinthians 11.26). Moreover, those who profane the body and blood of the Lord by failing to discern Christ in the eucharistic fellowship bring judgement upon themselves (1 Corinthians 11.27–9). *Koinonia* also features in the Johannine literature. In 1 John, for example, we read: 'We

---

[20] *Christifideles laici*, 18, Apostolic Exhortation on the Laity.

[21] See, for example, J. Reuman, '*Koinonia* in Scripture: Survey of Biblical Texts', in T.F. Best and G. Gassman (eds.), *On the Way to Fuller Koinonia*, Official Report of the Fifth World Conference on Faith and Order, Faith and Order Paper 166 (Geneva: World Council of Churches Publications, 1994), pp. 37–69.

proclaim to you what we have seen and heard, so that you may have fellowship with us. And our fellowship is with the Father and with his Son Jesus Christ' (1 John 1.3; cf. 1 John 1.7). The author speaks of a two-dimensional *koinonia*: first, the fellowship of the Father with his Son Jesus Christ, and second, and in consequence of this, the fellowship of Christians with one another. The fellowship of Christians with one another is grounded in the trinitarian fellowship revealed in Christ, and is a precondition for their participation in the latter.

Koinonia has become a key concept in recent ecumenical thinking about the nature of the Church. *The Unity of the Church as Koinonia: Gift and Calling*, the statement issued following the 1991 Canberra assembly of the World Council of Churches, identified the *koinonia* or unity of the Church with the trinitarian God's purposes for the whole of creation.[22] The opening paragraph described the Church as a foretaste of God's plan 'to gather the whole creation under the Lordship of Christ Jesus in whom, by the power of the Holy Spirit, all are brought into communion with God'. *Koinonia* also formed the principal theme of the fifth World Conference on Faith and Order held at Santiago de Compostela in 1993.[23] There is also clear evidence that this concept has emerged as the fundamental understanding of the Church in recent dialogues between different churches.[24]

The modern renaissance in trinitarian theology and its application to ecclesiology has undoubtedly played a key part in the development of communion ecclesiology. In his contribution to the Fifth World Conference on Faith and Order held at Santiago de Compostela in 1993 the

[22] See M. Kinnamon (ed.), *Signs of the Spirit* (Geneva and Grand Rapids: World Council of Churches Publications and Eerdmans, 1991), pp. 172–4.

[23] See Best and Gassman, *On the Way to Fuller Koinonia*.

[24] See, for example, *Fifth Forum on Bilateral Conversations*, Faith and Order Paper 156 (Geneva: World Council of Churches Publications, 1989), p. 46.

Orthodox theologian John Zizioulas points to the 1961 New Delhi Assembly of the World Council of Churches as marking a decisive turning-point.[25] At the latter the Council's basis was expanded to include reference to the Holy Trinity. Two years later the Faith and Order conference held at Montreal in 1963 stressed that the theology of the Church should be derived from the trinitarian understanding of God and not just from Christology. The Church is not just 'in Christ'. It is also 'in the Father' by the 'power of the Holy Spirit'. It is constituted as a communion or fellowship because it is founded upon the very life of God himself. As Zizioulas puts it:

> The fact that God reveals to us his existence as one of personal communion is decisive in our understanding of the nature of the Church. It implies that when we say that the Church is koinonia, we mean no other kind of communion but the very personal communion between the Father, the Son and the Spirit.[26]

As we have already indicated, alongside its use in modern ecumenical dialogue the concept of *koinonia* has also become a key element in the wider discussion of the concept of the Church. Communion and fellowship are increasingly being seen as fundamental to the being and identity of the Church. Communion is both the form and the basis of the eschatological community of salvation. It links the Church with God's purposes for the whole creation, his plan for the 'fullness of time'. Ecclesial communion is an anticipation of the end of history when God will become 'all in all'. It is not merely a hope for the future but the central and defining feature of the Church's life.[27]

[25] J. Zizioulas, 'The Church as Communion: A Presentation on the World Conference Theme' in Best and Gassman, *On the Way to Fuller Koinonia*, pp. 103–11.

[26] *On the Way to Fuller Koinonia*, p. 105.

[27] In his *Church, World and the Christian Life: Practical-Prophetic Ecclesiology* (Cambridge: Cambridge University Press, 2000), pp. 44–5, Nicholas M. Healey is sharply critical of the communion model, arguing that it represents an

Dennis Doyle provides us with a helpful summary of this approach to ecclesiology:

> Communion ecclesiology ... represents an attempt to move beyond the merely juridical and institutional understandings by emphasising the mystical, sacramental, and historical dimensions of the Church. It focuses on relationships, whether among the persons of the Trinity, among human beings and God, among the members of the Communion of Saints, among members of the parish, or among the bishops dispersed throughout the world. It emphasises the dynamic interplay between the Church universal and the local churches. Communion ecclesiology stresses that the Church is not simply the receiver of revelation, but as the Mystical Body of Christ is bound up with revelation itself.[28]

We might add to this that communion ecclesiology also stresses the eschatological character of the Church. The Church's *koinonia* is a sacramental anticipation of the reconciliation of all things in Christ. Its eucharistic life is a sign and instrument of the fellowship of God's kingdom. This was a key point in the second Anglican–Roman Catholic International Commission's (ARCIC II) discussion of the ecclesiology of communion. The Commission's agreed statement described the Church as a 'mystery' or

---

idealized view of the Church, divorced from the actual history of the Christian community. This is an over-simplistic reaction. The Church's history of division and conflict is not the end of the matter. The Church has both an historical and an eschatological existence. As the community of the Spirit the Church also exists from the *eschaton*. Its story is that of both Christ and the Holy Spirit. This is not an idealization against history. The Church's story is a participation in the divine engagement with history. Like the history of Jesus, the history of the Church unfolds from the resurrection. As we will see further on in this chapter, the ecclesiology of communion offers a way of exploring the eschatological dialectic between promise and fulfilment in the life of the Church. The Church is not identical with the kingdom but it proclaims the promise of the kingdom and, in its *koinonia*, already anticipates its fulfilment. It is simultaneously a sign and instrument of the hoped-for kingdom and a foretaste and anticipation of the fulfilment of the kingdom. Set within history it none the less has its existence from that which is beyond history.

[28] Doyle, *Communion Ecclesiology*, p. 12.

'sacrament'.[29] The Church was defined as:

> a visible sign which both points to and embodies our communion
> with God and with one another; as an instrument through which
> God effects this communion; and as a foretaste of the fullness of
> communion to be consummated when Christ is all in all.[30]

The sacramental model points up the fact that the Church
has its existence beyond itself in relation to both God and
the world. As a sacrament it signifies human incorporation
into the communion of the Son and the Father in the power
of the Holy Spirit, and it anticipates the world's final
communion in God. The Church is described as a sacrament
because it embodies the reality that it also signifies.

Sacramental language provides us with a helpful con-
ceptual vehicle for uncovering the dynamic character of
ecclesial *koinonia*. Sacramental signs have a double character.
They are related to created reality in one direction and in

---

[29] The sacramental model of the Church is gaining ground in Catholic
ecclesiology. See, for example, H. de Lubac, *Catholicism, Christ and the Common
Destiny of Man* (London: Burns and Oates, 1950), p. 28, who is usually credited
with having revived this way of understanding the Church; A. Dulles, *Models of
the Church* (Dublin: Gill and Macmillan, 1976), pp. 58–70; W. Kasper, *Theology
and Church* (London: SCM Press, (1989)), pp. 111–28; K. Rahner, *The Church
and the Sacraments* (London: Burns and Oates, 1974), pp. 11–75; 'Membership of
the Church According to the Teaching of Pius XII's Encyclical *Mystici Corporis
Christi*', in *Theological Investigations* (London: Darton, Longman & Todd, 1963),
vol. 2, pp. 1–88; *Foundations of Christian Faith* (London: Darton, Longman &
Todd; New York: Seabury, 1978), pp. 411–13; J. Ratzinger, *Principles of
Catholic Theology: Building Stones for a Fundamental Theology* (San Francisco:
Ignatius Press, 1987), pp. 44–54; E. Schillebeeckx, *Christ The Sacrament of
Encounter with God* (London: Sheed & Ward, 1963). While the sacramental
model has not received much attention outside Catholic ecclesiology, there is a
discussion of it by the Protestant theologian Eberhard Jüngel. See his 'The
Church as Sacrament?' in *Eberhard Jüngel: Theological Essays* (Edinburgh: T. & T.
Clark, 1989), pp. 189–213. It was also adopted by the Anglican theologian H.
Burn-Murdock in *Church, Continuity and Unity* (Cambridge: Cambridge Uni-
versity Press, 1945), pp. 31–7

[30] *Church as Communion: An Agreed Statement by the Second Anglican–Roman
Catholic International Commission* (London: Church House Publishing and
Catholic Truth Society, 1991), 17.

the other to the new order of salvation and redemption in Christ. As such they are symbols of human hope *and* signs of the promised fulfilment of *koinonia*. The Church too has this double character. It is a human society oriented both to this age and the yearning for salvation, and to the new age of God's kingdom. This is why, paradoxically, the Church signifies both the need for salvation and the reality of salvation in Christ.

There is a constant struggle in ecclesiology to maintain an appropriate balance between the twin orientations of the Church. One traditional way of doing this is to draw a distinction between the Church as a visible community of women and men and as an invisible reality of divine grace. According to this approach the true reality of the Church is said to reside in what lies concealed behind its public face. This conceptualization must ultimately be judged a failure. It polarizes the divine and human elements in the Church, and misrepresents its double orientation. The human and historical face of the Church is an essential element in its sacramental character. It is precisely as a visible community of men and women that it reveals the eschatological mystery of God's kingdom. Locating what is ultimately significant about the Church in what lies hidden from view is destructive of the very idea of the Church itself. As sacrament the Church is necessarily a human sign of the gift of divine grace.

The double character of the sacraments has generally been explained in ontological terms. The traditional Western distinction between *res* and *sacramentum* is an example of such an approach. The *sacramentum* is the external or visible sign of the sacrament. The *res* is the internal reality of the sacrament; the grace that gives the visible sign its salvific power. The difficulty with this distinction between the external form of a sacrament and its inner reality is that it depends upon the visible/invisible dualism noted above. This is one consequence of the use of ontological language.

When sacraments are conceptualized in terms of substantial presence, qualifications are needed in order to avoid this being seen as a 'capture' of the divine by fallen created reality. Hence the divine sacramental presence is qualified by describing it as a form of concealment within the visible sign. Eschatology offers a more promising vehicle for discussing the dual character of the sacraments.[31] It locates sacramental language in the grammar of event and promise rather than that of objects and things. The New Testament sets the two dominical sacraments within an eschatological prospect. John the Baptist contrasts his own baptism of repentance with Jesus' baptism with 'the Holy Spirit and with fire' (Matthew 3.11). Paul describes baptism as incorporation into the death and resurrection of Christ (Romans 6.3–4; cf., Colossians 2.12) and the institution narratives identify the Eucharist with the coming kingdom (Matthew 26.29; Mark 14.25; Luke 22.16, 18, 29f.). This eschatological prospect is reflected in the liturgical framing of the Eucharist in terms of *anamnesis* and *epiclesis*. In *anamnesis* the Church is enfolded in the mystery of Christ's life, death and resurrection. By invocation of the Holy Spirit the symbols of his passion become an anticipation of the fullness of the kingdom. The sacrament does not recall an event that exists only in the past. It celebrates and enacts the emergence of God's future in the resurrection of Christ. In the Eucharist we recall Jesus as the one who is to come. *Anamnesis* is, as John Zizioulas puts it, 'the memory of the future'.[32]

Identifying the Church in relation to the *eschaton* is one of the intractable problems of ecclesiology. There is always the

---

[31] For a fuller discussion of the eschatological approach to the sacraments see G. Wainwright, *Eucharist and Eschatology* (London: Epworth Press, 1971). See also my more detailed discussion of the points raised above in 'Foundations for an Ecclesiology of Ministry', in C. Hall, and R. Hannaford (eds.), *Order and Ministry* (Leominster: Gracewing, 1996), esp., pp. 39f.

[32] Zizioulas, *Being As Communion*, p. 180.

danger of misrepresenting the dynamic nature of the Church's constitution by the *eschaton*. We say too much or too little: representing the Church either as an absolute or final community or as merely a fallible community of women and men. Many have, for example, spoken of the Church as existing in the between-times, i.e. in the time between Christ's resurrection and the final resurrection of the dead. As a way of explaining the 'already' and 'not yet' nature of the Church's life, this fails to do full justice to its double character. It amounts to a fixing of the grounds of the Church's eschatological life *within* history. Although formed as a community of women and men set within history, the Church is constituted by the *eschaton*, which exists beyond history. We need a way of representing the fact that the Church is jointly constituted by its orientation to the community of women and men and to the new *koinonia* of the age to come.

One way forward is to speak of the Church's orientation to the *eschaton* in terms of the dialectic of promise and fulfilment. The Church is a sacrament of God's final gift of salvation because it signifies that gift as both promise and fulfilment. Promise and fulfilment are dialectically related in the sense that they are mutually constitutive modes of the kingdom's presence in the life and ministry of the Church. The Church exists in the mode of promise in the sense that it points to that which it also awaits. It exists in the mode of fulfilment because in declaring what is promised the Church also anticipates the fulfilment of that promise. This approach to the double character of the Church is consistent with the claim the Church is constituted by the *eschaton*. In Christ, specifically his resurrection, human yearning for fulfilment is transformed into promise, becoming also thereby an anticipation of the fulfilment of that promise. Promise and fulfilment both owe their origin to the preaching of the kingdom. In terms of the former the Church is a sign of the true substance of human expectation and hope. In terms of the latter it is a sign of the ultimacy of God's kingdom.

The Church's ministry of proclamation provides us with an illustration of this dialectic. When the Church proclaims the good news of the kingdom it clearly acts under the dialectic of promise, pointing forward to the promised fulfilment of all things. However, in declaring the promise of God, the Church acts with authority because it already experiences in its own life the substance of that promise, and thus corresponds also to the dialectic of fulfilment. So, for example, the writer of St John declares that when Christians speak of Christ and what he has done they do so in the power of the one who is to come, the Holy Spirit (John 14.26; 16.13). Similarly, the author of Mark's Gospel states that when Christians fulfil their ministry of proclamation it is not they who speak but the Holy Spirit (Mark 13.11), the same Spirit whose advent is the principal sign of God's kingdom come in power. The Church's spirit-filled declaration of the promise of the kingdom is also a manifestation of the power and presence of the end times.

If the Church is structured in relation to both promise and fulfilment, then hope is the characteristic form of its life. Hope is precisely the hope of fulfilment, but it is constituted as such by being the eagerness and longing of those who *await* what is promised. Conversely, since there must be grounds for hope, it can only be present if there is already anticipation and foretaste. Hope is at the same time a sign of present incompleteness – one does not hope for what one already has – and of the confident and faithful expectation of the completion to come (Romans 8.24–5). It is the chaacteristic form of life of those who live under the dialectic of promise and fulfilment.

In its *koinonia* the Church is a sacramental sign of God's plan for the reconciliation of all things. It is, as various theologians have put it, the world viewed from its end. In so far as it points to the end of all things, it is a sign of what is ultimate and final, but it is not itself – at least, not yet – the ultimate or final community of men and women. It might be more appropriate to describe the Church 'militant here on earth' as a penultimate reality, but more of that in due course. The Church's existence in relation to the *eschaton* cannot be reduced wholly to either one or other of the two modes of promise and fulfilment. As a community existing under the dialectic of promise the Church represents the world waiting 'with eager longing for the revealing of the sons of God' (Romans 8.19). At the same time, as the community already in possession of the first fruits of the Spirit (Romans 8.23), it exists under the dialectic of fulfilment, and thus represents the world ahead of itself.

Drawing a distinction between the visible and the invisible Church and locating its 'true' character in the latter is a particular manifestation of the failure to discern the dynamic relationship of the Church to God's eschatological kingdom. As a solution to the problem of representing the double orientation of the Church to the kingdom it fails because the historical community of faith is relativized, and its soteriological significance is misrepresented. The eschatological priority of God's kingdom does not mean that the Church's mission is rendered impossible until it is perfected. Suggesting as much results from an exclusive focus on the dialectic of fulfilment, ignoring altogether the sense in which the Church is also the community of promise. Equally questionable is the position of those opponents of the Episcopal Ministry Act of Synod 1993, who reject its provision for extended episcopal care as inconsistent with the principle of episcopal communion. They insist that one is either in or out of communion with one's bishop and that any compromise is theologically impossible. It is true that for many Anglicans, along with the rest of catholic Christianity, the local expression of the Church is the eucharistic community gathered around its bishop. However, to suggest that communion at this level is a matter of 'all or nothing' is inconsistent with the Church's double orientation to the kingdom. Since the Church is dialectically related to the kingdom, it is not possible to identify any single feature of its life as an unambiguous manifestation of either promise or fulfilment. But this is precisely what is implied in this case. The *koinonia* of bishop and people, unlike other manifestations of ecclesial *koinonia*, is taken to represent the Church only after the mode of fulfilment. The difficulty with any attempt to absolutize communion in one feature or moment of the Church's existence is that this leads to an inevitable relativization of other manifestations of communion. It appears that we are once again confronted with the kind of polarization that informs the invisible/visible Church divide. Absolutizing any aspect of the Church's life, and treating it as a signal manifestation of the Church's orientation to the fulfilment of the age to come, misrepresents its double character. The *koinonia* of bishop and people is undoubtedly a key element in catholic ecclesiology, but its significance is fatally misrepresented if it is treated as an exception to the Church's constitution after the dialectic of fulfilment *and* promise. It too is both a sign and an anticipation of the coming kingdom of reconciliation and peace.

Koinonia *and Ontology*

We can make the same point in a slightly different way. The debate about communion, both in general and in the particular case of the Act of Synod, tends to draw on the language of ontology. Many of those who regard the ordination of women to the priesthood and episcopate as a departure from apostolic tradition have claimed that they are no longer in communion with their fellow Anglicans. Being in communion, they would argue, is a matter of all or nothing. Against such clear-cut affirmations, and in partial defence of its suggested arrangements, the Eames commission insisted that the notion of simply being 'in communion' or 'out of communion' is insufficient.[33] Apart from appealing to the evidence of growing ecumenical convergence the theological grounds of this position are not spelt out in the report, but our analysis suggests that it can be by appealing to the dynamic grounds of ecclesial communion. The polarization of views on this matter represents an unhelpful ontologization of the language of *koinonia*. Communion is a feature of the mission of the Church and not only of its being or identity. It is the Church's task as well as its gift.

On the side of ontology the Gospel of John grounds the fellowship or communion of believers in the relationship between the Father and the Son:

> I do not pray for these only, but also for those who believe in me through their word, that they may all be one; even as thou, Father, art in me, and I in thee, that they also may be in us, so that the world may believe that thou hast sent me. The glory which thou hast given me I have given to them, that they may be one even as we are one, I in them and thou in me, that they may become perfectly one, so that the world may know that thou hast sent me and hast loved them even as thou hast loved me. (John 17.20–3)

It is certainly clear that John lays enormous stress on the unity of the Church and in that sense on its structure and form. The Church's being as a communion is said to reflect the unity of the Son and the Father. However, the Johannine vision of communion does not support a sharp polarization between questions of function or purpose and being or nature. John also insists that ecclesial communion has a purpose, namely, 'that the world may believe,' and this links communion firmly with the mission of the Church. Communion relates both to the being and the mission of the

---

[33] 'The First Report', *The Eames Commission: The Official Reports*, para. 56. Excerpted and used by permission as before.

Church. The Church is constituted as a communion whose mission is to proclaim the saving work of Christ in drawing all things into fellowship or communion with the Father.

The tendency to polarize the discussion of communion so that it is seen either in terms of ontology or in terms of mission arises in part from a failure to note the eschatological character of the Church. The Johannine High Priestly prayer, quoted above, continues as follows:

> Father, I desire that they also, whom thou hast given me, may be with me where I am, to behold my glory which thou hast given me in thy love for me before the foundation of the world. (John 17.24)

Koinonia is already Christ's saving gift to the Church but it is such as an anticipation of the glory that will be his final gift. While time remains – and, as a community that already shares in the first fruits of salvation – the Church is to seek an ever-closer conformity to the divine unity of the Father and the Son. As a manifestation of the eschatologically decisive saving action of God, the Church's communion is both a present reality and a hope for the future. Communion is both the gift and the calling of the Christian community. The Church is called, paradoxically, to an ever more perfect realization of what it already is. Alongside the *koinonia* that is constitutive of the Church's identity we must also speak of a corresponding discipleship of *koinonia*. As those who live by the Spirit, who draws men and women into the fellowship of the one God, Christians are also called to walk by the same Spirit (Galatians 5.25; cf., Colossians 2.6).

The Act of Synod and the Discipleship of Koinonia

So far we have approached the question of the provisions of the Act of Synod negatively, by challenging the absolutized view of episcopal *koinonia* held by some of those who oppose the measure. Is it possible to pass a positive judgement on its proposals for the establishment of extended episcopal care? I want to begin by quoting from a key passage in the introduction to the Eames report. In commending the report to the Anglican Communion the commission appeals for a spirit of 'respect' and 'courtesy':

> When differences of principle and practice result in tension, debate and pain, such a spirit will create a profound unity and communion beyond that which the world knows. If those who find the exclusion of women from the priesthood and episcopate contrary to an understanding of God's justice and the meaning of the Incarnation, and those who find their inclusion an unacceptable development of the apostolic ministry can come together to share each other's burdens and sufferings, then the Anglican Communion will have learned something of the meaning of communion with the God who suffers. And we shall have something to say about the unity of Christians and the unity of all humankind.[34]

This invitation to seek a communion that encompasses differences in principle and practice will be dismissed by some as an example of Anglican woolly-mindedness, making a virtue out of an unfortunate necessity. However, such an appeal cannot be dismissed so lightly. As we have suggested, the ministry of the Church is not rendered impossible until it is perfected. On the contrary, it is in its very incompleteness and in an accompanying awareness of dependence upon God's promise of fulfilment that the Church bears witness to his love and mercy. St Paul understood this well, recognizing that his weakness was a sign of the efficacy of God's grace (cf. 2 Corinthians 12.9; 4.7–12). There is an important sense in which 'what is lacking' in the life of the Church also serves the mission of God. The suggestion is not that sin and disorder in the Church should increase in order that grace might abound. Our claim rather is that the desire to avoid schism and

---

[34] *The Eames Commission: The Official Reports*, p. 13. Excerpted and used by permission as before.

embrace differences within the context of a discipleship of *koinonia* is consistent with the Church's witness to the primary sufficiency of grace. The Church's potency as a sacramental sign depends entirely upon the power of God's love. It is only when we are weak and recognise our incompleteness that we know our need of God, and hence bear witness to the gratuitous nature of salvation. To say otherwise is dangerously near to suggesting that the Church ceases to be the Church when it manifests incompleteness. The Church is always both promise and fulfilment. In this sense its very incompleteness, in signifying 'what is lacking', serves the mystery of God's will, pointing to the fulfilment that it too hopes and yearns for.

The desire to embrace divisions within a wider vision of communion has led some ecumenists to describe the various historic Christian churches as 'provisional'.[35] This is an unfortunate term, suggesting that the Church in this age is not already an anticipation of the fulfilment of the age to come. If the Church is merely provisional, it is difficult to see how it can be regarded as a community that already owes its present existence entirely to the future. It is true that the Church is also orientated towards this age and the yearning of men and women for fulfilment, but in this too it is constituted by the *eschaton*. In the new relationships inaugurated by Christ, human yearning is transformed into hope, constituting the Church as the community of promise. We have described promise and fulfilment dialectically because both are simultaneous manifestations of the Church's constitution by the advent of God's kingdom of peace and reconciliation. As promise the Church points beyond itself: as fulfilment it anticipates in its own life that which is promised. In both cases it is constituted by God's kingdom. As the world ahead of itself the Church

---

[35] See, for example, C. Duquoc, *Provisional Churches* (London: SCM Press, 1986).

exists entirely from the ultimate and definitive future.

Although the Church is entirely defined by its relationship to the kingdom, it is clear that it is not yet the ultimate community of the kingdom. Indeed we have even spoken of 'what is lacking' in its life as also at the service of the kingdom. Paradoxically the Church signifies both the gift of salvation and the need for salvation. The Church already anticipates the fulfilment to come, but awaits its final consummation. Rather than describing the historic churches as provisional it is more appropriate to speak of the Church as a penultimate human community. The Church is penultimate because, even in its incompleteness, the Christian community is defined by its relationship to the ultimate. It is only in awareness of the ultimate that human life can be transformed into a discipleship of hope and thus become a *diakonia*[36] of the kingdom. Describing the Church as provisional exaggerates its contingency, ignoring the sense in which its life already represents the transformation of human yearning into the hope and promise of the ultimate.

The Church is a penultimate community in the sense that it exists entirely at the service of the ultimate. It is a community of men and women struggling to realize in their own lives the obedience of faith, which is the *koinonia* of the Holy Spirit. In this light it is possible to offer a favourable judgement on the Anglican Communion's struggle to maintain unity in the face of internal divisions over doctrine and practice. Is it not possible to see in, for example, the provision of extended episcopal care a genuine act of *koinonia* discipleship on the part of Anglicans? From the point of view of the theology of ministry this appears

---

[36] *Diakonia* is usually translated as 'ministry' or 'service' but see the important new study of this New Testament word and its cognates in J.N. Collins, *Diakonia: Re-interpreting the Ancient Sources* (Oxford and New York: Oxford University Press, 1990).

anomalous, a compromise designed as a concession to circumstances, but seen against the wider background of an ecclesiology of *koinonia* it is possible to view it more positively as representing a recognition of the penultimacy of the Church. It is in a small way an action in the service of the ultimate state of humanity – 'that they all may be one'.

6

RECEPTION AND THE ACT OF SYNOD

Christopher Hill

I will consider the doctrine of reception and the Act of Synod by *first* considering the classical doctrine of reception and the subsequent modern development of ecumenical reception; *second*, by examining how the doctrine of reception came to be applied to the ordination of women within the Anglican Communion; *third*, by making some observations on the actual application of the doctrine of reception to the ordination of women; *fourth*, by commenting on the state of communion between Christians in a time of reception; and *fifth*, by looking at the Act of Synod in the light of the examined understanding of reception.

1. 'The classical idea of reception' is a phrase used by Metropolitan John Zizioulas,[1] taken up and helpfully developed by Dr Bill Rusch in his book *Reception: An Ecumenical Opportunity*.[2] To quote Rusch: 'Classical reception is reception as it was understood before the rise of the ecumenical movement; ecumenical reception is reception as it is understood since the increase of ecumenical dialogue during the 1960s. Although there are similarities between the two concepts of reception, there are also significant differences.'[3] The application of a doctrine of reception to the ordination of women is different yet again to both

---

[1] John Zizioulas, 'The Theological Problem of Reception', *Centro pro Unione Bulletin* 26 (1984): 4–6.

[2] William G. Rusch, *Reception: An Ecumenical Opportunity* (Philadelphia: Fortress Press, 1988).

[3] Ibid., p. 29.

classical reception and ecumenical reception. But there are, I believe, important parallels.

Classical reception is a large subject with a growing literature. Rusch's summary is an excellent summary and builds on the classical study of reception made by Yves Congar, OP, 'Reception as an Ecclesiological Reality'.[4] I will summarize those parts of Congar's article which have relevance for the ordination of women (though of course Congar did not himself apply them to the ordination of women). Congar examines the view of the Jesuit patristic scholar Aloys Grillmeier, who traces the patristic reception of the doctrine of Christ in his three-volume *Christ in Christian Tradition*.[5] Grillmeier follows certain German[6] legal theory and holds that real reception is always *exogenous*. That is to say reception can properly be applied only where a doctrine, practice or canonical decision is accepted by a *separate* church. That is to say the thing to be received comes from outside – it is *exogenous*. Congar cites a theoretical Nestorian acceptance of the Council of Ephesus, or the Monophysites accepting Chalcedon, as clear examples of this. It is worthwhile remembering that ecumenical reception clearly could come into this definition. But Congar says, 'this way of looking at reception seems too narrow'. Congar continues:

> Of course there must always be a certain distance, a certain difference, between the party which gives and the party which receives. But if one remains within the framework of the one Church, its nature or its firm requirement of communion prevents the difference from being total ... But history offers an

---

[4] Yves Congar, 'Reception as an Ecclesiological Reality', *Concilium* 7.8, ed. Giuseppe Alberigo and Anton Weiler (London: Burns & Oates, 1972).

[5] Aloys Grillmeier, *Christ in Christian Tradition*, vol. 1, trans. J. S. Bowden (London: Mowbray, 1965); vol. 2, trans. Pauline Allen and John Cawte (London: Mowbray, 1987).

[6] Aloys Grillmeier, 'Konzil und Rezeption. Methodische Bemerkungen zu einem Thema der ökumenischen Diskussion', *Theologie und Philosophie* 45 (1970): 321–52.

enormous array of actual 'receptions', and theories of reception within the one Church.[7]

My second point from Congar is that classical conciliar reception was neither quick nor obvious. Nicaea (325) was received only after 56 years of contention, rival synods, imperial intervention and violence. Quarrels more or less came to an end only at the subsequent Council of Constantinople (381). *That* Council came to be received as ecumenical only because its creed was received as of Nicene faith. Its constituency was *not* ecumenical, as St Ambrose hotly pointed out.

Third, as Congar reminds us, there is 'non-reception'. Most famously the Council of Chalcedon was, and is still, not received by the Monophysite churches: the Copts, the Armenians and the Syrian and the Indian churches. Congar also notes the problem of the 'non-reception' of Trent by the Protestant churches: 'non-reception (can even) . . . affirm that decisions have been null since their making'.[8] Though 'non-reception' does not necessarily always mean this.

Congar examines the question of ecumenicity and the related question of who recognizes councils. He sympathizes with the Orthodox standpoint that it is not the legal correctness of a council that gives it authenticity, 'but the content of its teaching'. The essential thing was to detect in the councils the faith of the apostles transmitted by the Church. The important thing was not the number of the participants nor the legality of its procedure but the content of its decisions. In other words reception does not equate to a legally made or even legally binding decision. Reception 'does not confer validity, but affirms, acknowledges and attests that this matter is for the good of the Church; because it concerns a decision (dogma, canons, ethical rules) that should ensure the good of the Church.

---

[7] Congar, 'Reception as an Ecclesiological Reality', pp. 44–5.
[8] Ibid., p. 66, quoting Paul Hinschius.

This is why the reception of a Council is practically identical with its efficacy.'[9]

So much for the moment for that seminal article by Congar, though I shall return to it. Bill Rusch eloquently expands the newer usage of reception in relation to the ecumenical movement, particularly the results of the multinational and bilateral dialogues. I shall simply quote two examples: the *Lima Text* of the Faith and Order Commission of the WCC and the *Final Report* of ARCIC I. As these documents are reasonably familiar I shall not go into great detail or background.

When the *Lima Text* was finalized in January 1982 it was commended to the churches by the Vancouver assembly of the WCC in 1985. The terms of this commendation were expressed by the Faith and Order Commission in terms of four questions, the first of which asked: 'the extent to which your church can recognize in this text the faith of the Church through the ages'. This was a test of antiquity.

Similarly, though not identically, at the conclusion of its final session in 1986 at the end of a long ten-day meeting, the members of ARCIC drew up a question to the churches of the Anglican Communion and to the Roman Catholic Church in the name of the two co-chairmen: 'We ask whether the Agreed Statements ... are consonant in substance with the faith of Anglicans/Roman Catholics.' This was a test of present faith.

The subsequent story of these two major ecumenical documents is well documented. It is clearly a story largely of reception, with some non-reception. It is also obvious that reception does not end when an authoritative body or person, be it General Synod, Lambeth Conference or on the other hand the Congregation for the Doctrine of the Faith have had their say. Ecumenical reception is a *process* and, as with the classical reception of councils, must not be iden-

[9] Ibid.

tified as complete simply because a synod or council has spoken. Bill Rusch helpfully spells out the many stages of ecumenical reception in his book already quoted; I shall not now repeat these stages, as my point is simply to show that it has many common features with classical reception. But what of its application to the ordination of women?

2. It is well known that the Eames Commission makes considerable use of the concept of reception in its work on women in the episcopate. Eames did not invent this (admittedly new) usage. The Lambeth Conference of 1988 passed its famous Resolution 1 in which it invited the Archbishop of Canterbury, in consultation with the (other) Primates, to appoint a commission which would among other things: 'ensure that the process of reception includes continuing consultation with other Churches...'

This oblique reference to ecumenical reception is made clearer in the Report on Mission and Ministry, para. 133, which was the context of the Resolution. Here it was said that 'the concept of reception has affected consideration of the ordination of women to the presbyterate and episcopate' and 'in the process of reception the issue continues to be tested until it is clearly accepted or not accepted by the whole Church'.

Behind this language lay the work of the Primates Working Party on Women and the Episcopate, the *Grindrod Report* (known after the Working Party's Chairman, Archbishop John Grindrod of Brisbane). They met twice, in January and July 1987, in preparation for the Lambeth Conference of the following year. In an important section on the process of decision-making in the universal Church a significant paragraph was devoted to a process of reception with regard to the ordination of women. After a paragraph setting out an ecumenical argument for restraint, a following paragraph dealt with the option of going forward to ordain women to the episcopate. It is here that a theology of reception is first developed in relation to the ordination of women. I quote the whole of paragraph 85:

> However at the present time if a decision is to be made the only effective level at which it can be made is at Provincial level but with due regard given to consultation with all the Provinces through the ACC and the Lambeth Conference and with due listening to sister churches. Should a Province, after due consultation proceed to consecrate a woman as bishop then that decision would still have to be tested in the universal Church. As with other developments of faith and order such a development would have to be affirmed by the people of God under the guidance of the Holy Spirit. A long range and far-reaching process of reception by the whole Church would lie ahead. Until a process of reception is reasonably settled the issue of the ordination of women to the episcopate, as indeed the ordination of women to the presbyterate, would remain open to discussion. A continuing discussion between Provinces and between churches in the ecumenical movement would be appropriate. We are already in bilateral and multilateral conversations with our sister churches and look forward to exchanges on the subject. It might be possible for some who remain agnostic, or who are even opposed to the consecration of women to remain in communion with Provinces that consecrated women, and even to share collegially with women, providing all understand the practice within the perspective of such a continuing and open process of reception. However, it needs to be recognised that there is a very particular problem when what is being put to the test in the reception process is not just a doctrine to be discussed but a doctrine that is already embodied in persons which touch and affect the very bond of communion.

The *Grindrod Report* later expanded on reception in the following way (paras. 91 and 92):

> 'Reception' is a long and spiritual process involving both official response by the synods and councils of the Church 'at the highest level of authority'. It also involves a longer and more widespread process of reception. Conciliar or synodical decisions, themselves emerging from widespread consultation and episcopal guidance, have to be received. If in the course of time the Church as a whole receives a synodical decision this would be an additional or final sign that it may be judged to be in accordance with God's will for

the Church (*Final Report of ARCIC, Authority I*, para. 6; *Elucidation*, para. 3; *Authority II*, para. 25). The people of God, under the guidance of the Holy Spirit, have to be involved in forming the mind of the Church in matters affecting the faith of the Church. Within this process the authority of those exercising leadership, individually, and corporately, is not a formal or imposed one. It is an authority supported and accepted by the involvement of the whole fellowship.

Whenever a matter is tested by the Church there is necessarily an openness about the question. The continuing communion of Christians with one another in faith and worship maintains the underlying unity of the Church while the reception process is at work. The openness needs to be recognised and accepted by those on both sides of the debate. There needs to be an openness to the possibility of the new thing being accepted by the Church or rejected by the Church. It also entails a willingness to live with diversity throughout the 'reception' process.

Reception is a long range and far reaching process in which the whole Church seeks to recognise and affirm confidently the one faith ... and confidently to lay hold of the new life which that faith promises (*Gathered for Life: The Official Report of the Vancouver Assembly*, WCC 1983).

The reception process cannot be hurried; it demands patience and listening on both sides and calls for generosity of spirit. Sensitivity and mutual caring is even more called for when what is in question is matters of faith embodied in the ministry of women and men. The ideal of unity and the quest for truth may be pursued and upheld as the process of reception is worked out.

The Eames Commission which followed the Lambeth Conference of 1988 built upon this foundation. Its First Report spoke of an 'open process of reception' and, significantly, a reception process following any synodical decision to move forward with the ordination of women to the priesthood and episcopate, where still there remains a body of dissent: 'The fact that a synod has reached a decision does not foreclose the matter. Both sides need to work hard to ensure that the process of reception continues to be as open as possible, recognising that synodal decisions may indeed come to be overwhelmingly affirmed, or on the other hand, equally as overwhelmingly rejected.'[10]

The Primates Meeting in 1989 endorsed the Eames Commission, speaking appreciatively of its 'analysis of the process of discernment and reception'.[11]

In its Second Report the Eames Commission continued to speak of an 'open process of reception', but it is in its Third Report that a more extended treatment of reception is given, putting it into its 'classical' context. I quote:

> In each age the Church receives and re-expresses the apostolic faith and discipline, and re-orders its life for the renewal and effectiveness of mission. Part of what is understood to be involved in this process of reception and transmission is the acceptance in one part of the Church of liturgical practices or innovative developments in matters of doctrine and discipline originating elsewhere. The process leading to the finalisation of the canon of Scripture is an obvious example of this kind of development. The development of creeds is another.
>
> Indeed, the New Testament evidence itself supports that different, and sometimes logically competing formulations and credal definitions emerged in different parts of the primitive Church, largely independent of one another. Inevitably, different patterns of ministry and disciplines of Christian behaviour often flourished independently in isolated and scattered places. The process of harmonization, involving the integrating of disparate elements into one congruous and universally accepted, if not entirely uniform, pattern was often extended over a period of centuries.[12]

Later in the same Report a whole section is devoted to reception. This particularly sets reception in its modern ecumenical context. Reception in this section is stressed as a continuing process; it is not effortless or painless and it can

---

[10] Eames Commission, First Report, para. 44, in *Women in the Anglican Episcopate: Theology Guidelines and Practice, The Eames Commission and Monitoring Group Reports* (Toronto: Anglican Book Centre, 1998).

[11] Primates Meeting, 1989, para. 96. See *Women in the Anglican Episcopate*, pp. 46–9.

[12] Eames Commission, Third Report, paras 169–70.

be difficult and time-consuming. Examples are quoted from both New Testament (the Logos doctrine and the admission of gentiles) and Early Church history (the first councils). The Reformation is acknowledged to have been a rediscovery of the gospel. Even after synod or council there is need for further discernment by the faithful. In the meantime space needs to be made for those of differing views and practices.

The Fourth Report in 1997 (from the Eames Monitoring Group rather than the whole Commission) also devoted a whole section to reception. It quoted extensively from the *Grindrod Report* already noted.

3. I now make some observations on the bearing of both 'classical' and 'ecumenical' reception in relation to the ordination of women.

(i) A broad view of reception suggests that there can be reception both within a single communion and between divided communions. It is therefore an appropriate concept to apply to matters of division within a communion. To defend this I refer to my quotation from Congar *rejecting* Grillmeier's narrower understanding that a proper reception can only be spoken of between separated churches.

(ii) Reception, either classical or ecumenical, is neither quick nor necessarily obvious at the time. We cannot, or should not, therefore set formal time constraints. An extreme example (cited by Congar) is the Council of Orange of 529 on justification, which was received and reiterated by the Council of Trent only some one thousand years later! Or in Christian ethics one can find sporadic Christian opposition to slavery during the patristic period, but it is only in modern times that a Christian consensus has emerged – largely without formal conciliar or synodical statements.

(iii) The possibility of 'non-reception' is also part of the understanding of reception. This can mean simply that the time is not ripe or opportune or culturally appropriate; it can also mean that a decision or definition was definitely wrong. Church history is littered with councils (and popes!) which have erred. There are also those difficult bits of church history where culture gets in the way of a clear decision. The story of the reception and non-reception of the Chalcedonian Definition is the story of two anthropologies (from Antioch and Alexandria respectively) which necessitated apparently conflicting Christological formulations to expound true faith in Christ.

(iv) Reception is never equated with legal process. Indeed in both classical and ecumenical understandings of reception the process of reception is merely reaching a particular (though important) moment when conciliar or synodical endorsement is given (or refused). To claim anything else is to risk the improbable claim of infallibility for synods – as Anglicans reject any such thing for councils and popes, this would be rather inconsistent! Nevertheless, once reception indicates the authenticity of a particular decision through general acceptance by the wider Church, we can, without claiming infallibility, discern that God did indeed guide the Church by his Spirit at that earlier point of decision-making. But this is neither automatic nor juridical.

(v) Though the classical doctrine of reception is mostly concerned with conciliar definitions, this is not exclusively the case. Congar notes the 'reception' of the canon of Scripture and liturgical reception. Further exploration needs to be done in the matter of the reception of *practice*. The emergence of the 'four-fold' eucharistic action from the 'seven-fold' action[13] when the Eucharist was still incorporated in a 'Passover'-style meal is an interesting, major and universal example of reception completely unencumbered by formal decision. Was it originally a local Corinthian development in response to St Paul's criticism of the *agape*?

[13] The thesis of Dom Gregory Dix, OSB, in *The Shape of the Liturgy* (Westminster: Dacre Press, 1947).

More to the point in relation to the ordination of women is the equally unconciliar emergence and development of the three-fold order of the apostolic ministry (bishops, presbyters and deacons) from the two-fold shape (bishops/presbyters and deacons) which is apparent in the Pastoral Epistles and in Clement of Rome (writing to Corinth). The Ignatian (Antiochene) pattern of the monarchical bishop very soon became universal, but it does appear to have been a *development* in order which then received universal reception. And there was some long-term resistance to this in Alexandria, as is well known from Jerome and the Alexandrine practice of presbyteral ordinations of bishops even when Alexandria had adopted 'episcopacy'.[14] From the modern ecumenical understanding of reception comes the interesting question of how divided or unrecognized ministries can be mutually received: for example, how can a singly ordered Reformation ministry be received by a church which possesses the traditional three-fold order and *vice versa*.

4. How does what I have been saying about reception relate to the question of communion? What does the classical history of reception tell us about communion during a time of reception? At first sight the answer looks negative. Orthodox and Arians were not in communion, even Semi-Arians were out of communion with Athanasius. But there may be a danger of looking only at the reception of the Nicene definition. Another story can be told of the long and complex history of the reception and non-reception of the Chalcedonian definition. Work done by the Pro Oriente Institute and others in relation to ecumenical reconciliation between the Oriental Orthodox churches, the Orthodox and

[14] For an account of the development of order at this period see: Henry Chadwick, *The Early Church* (Harmondsworth: Penguin Books, 1967), pp. 45–53.

the Western churches (particularly the Roman Catholic Church) is increasingly showing that in many places communion was never absolutely severed. Indeed 'on the ground' there was a *de facto* sacramental relationship, especially in Syria and Persia (under Islamic hegemony) and in India. Another case in point is the separation between East and West. In spite of the notorious Bull of Excommunication proclaimed by Cardinal Humbert in *Hagia Sophia* in 1054, in which a number of Eastern practices were denounced as well as omission of the *filioque*, contemporary ecumenical research sponsored by the Roman Catholic–Orthodox dialogue commission has increasingly shown that before and after 1054 there was not really a total break in communion. 'Interrupted communion' has been a phrase used by ecumenical historians. It is well known that Pope Paul VI and Pope John Paul II have regularly used the phrase 'almost perfect communion'[15] to describe the relationship between East and West. I believe this historical research is relevant and helpful as we consider the 'impaired' communion which the Eames Commission spoke of as now characterizing the Anglican Communion. In a process of reception, whether as in the troubled history of the Council of Chalcedon or between the Eastern and Western churches, there are *degrees* of communion. *But we are not out of communion.* A process of reception may entail less than perfect communion, or less than full juridical communion, until the matter is ultimately resolved; but it is wrong to speak of being 'out of communion' during a process of reception.

I have cited Congar more than once. Some years ago, in 1978, there took place at Versailles (in the Reformed Deaconess House at Reuilly, which has more recently given its name to the *Reuilly Common Statement*) an official

---

[15] For example, by Paul VI in 1971, cf. Edward Yarnold, *They are in Earnest: Christian Unity in the Statements of Paul VI, John Paul I, John Paul II* (Slough: St Paul Publications, 1982), p. 99.

Anglican–Roman Catholic consultation on the ordination of women. Its precise subject was whether churches which do ordain women and those which do not can have a sacramental relationship. This was just after the official Roman Catholic Declaration against the ordination of women *Inter insigniores* (1976). The *Versailles Statement* went only to the Lambeth Conference of 1978; it was never published, due to Vatican sensitivity. But its leading member on the Roman Catholic side was Congar himself. He helped draft the following paragraph and was himself the author of the key sentence about the Roman Catholic position:

> Two things have been seen as ground for hope. First there is the fact that those Anglican churches which have proceeded to ordain women to the presbyterate have done so in the conviction that they have not departed from the traditional understanding of apostolic ministry (expressed for example in the Canterbury Statement of the Anglican–Roman Catholic International Commission). In the second place there is the fact that the recent Roman Catholic Declaration does not affirm explicitly that this matter is *de jure divino*. These facts would seem not to exclude the possibility of future developments.[16]

For Congar the non-ordination of women could not be *de jure divino*, therefore he would not rule out the possibility of a sacramental relationship between churches which did and churches which did not ordain women. This must also have a bearing on the sacramental relationship between Anglican groups or churches which do or do not ordain women to the presbyterate and episcopate.

5.   How do we therefore assess the *Episcopal Ministry Act of Synod*?

It may help if I speak first of where I have come from. We all have our convictions, perspectives and prejudices.

[16] For this see further C.J. Hill, in Alyson Peberdy (ed.), *Women Priests?* (Basingstoke: Marshall Pickering, 1988).

Although I was opposed to the ordination of women to the priesthood for ecumenical, that is to say ecclesiological reasons, the Church of England having officially reached its decision, and having actually canonically ordained, women to the presbyterate, I fully accept what the Church has done and intends to do in the ordination of women. I have shared in the ordination of women first as a priest and also as a bishop within the Lichfield diocese. I have also licensed and instituted women priests to parishes in my Episcopal Area. My opposition to the ordination of women up until the vote had been not on the grounds that women cannot be ordained to the presbyterate (or indeed to the episcopate in principle) but that as the Church of England has consistently claimed not to have a ministry of its own, but to share in the threefold ministry of the undivided Church, it was not for us to make this development/extension/change unilaterally in isolation from the other churches which also share this catholic ministry. But I am not of the view that a church which makes such a change to the ministry ceases to be a church; in a divided Christendom there is sometimes no way of change other than unilaterally. Nor am I of the opinion that such a church suddenly loses the authenticity of its sacramental life. Church history is littered with examples of particular churches making considerable changes in matters of faith and order without losing their ecclesiality.[17] The Donatist thesis (i.e. that sacrilegious actions, or a church condoning or conniving with such sacrilegious actions by 'soft' discipline, cause a church to

---

[17] e.g. the Western addition of the Filioque clause, in Spain, Gaul, and finally Rome; or the gradual imposition of celibacy on all clerics in the West. Though it is often said that celibacy is 'merely disciplinary', it is clearly *more* than this for contemporary Roman Catholicism. Another range of examples would be the wide variation in the number of accepted sacraments at different times in church history and as between East, West and the Orientals; especially noteworthy is the variety in the accepted form and matter of the sacraments, especially Confirmation, over the centuries. There has also, significantly, been wide variety in the matter of the minor orders, especially in the East.

cease to be a church) was decisively rejected by Augustine and the Church Catholic some considerable time ago. I see no reason for doubting that the Catholic Church was right and the Donatist Church wrong.

I therefore believe the Church Catholic is indeed in a continuing process of reception in relation to the ordination of women as priests. I mean by this reception in its theological sense as outlined above: the Holy Spirit within the whole people of God, over a period of time, perhaps considerable time, accepting or rejecting a development or decision made by an authoritative body or person within the Church.[18] Unless and until there is such a moral certainty, we have not yet arrived at the *consensus fidelium*, and there must be thus room for dissent and doubt, and leeway if necessary for pastoral provision such as is provided for by the Episcopal Ministry Act of Synod 1993.[19]

[18] Cf. *The Eames Commission Monitoring Group Report* to the Lambeth Conference 1998, especially the earlier *Grindrod Report*, paras 91, 92, as quoted above.

[19] Cf. The Eames Commission, First Report, para. 55. 'From an ecclesiological perspective such a scheme can be defended, as a necessary and strictly extraordinary anomaly in preference to schism, if certain conditions are met. Dissenting priests and congregations must, for their part, not go as far as to refuse canonical recognition to their diocesan bishop or to say they are not in communion with their ordinary. This would mean that their position would fall short of maintaining that the Church could never admit women to the priesthood or episcopate. But their position could be expressed as a legitimate hesitancy to affirm the ordination of women to the priesthood and episcopate while the matter is in debate in a continuing open process of reception within the Anglican Communion and the universal Church. Bishops and dioceses who accept and endorse the ordination of women to the priesthood and episcopate would need to recognise, that within a genuinely open process of reception, there must still be room for those who disagree. Such bishops and dioceses would need to understand the problem of the uncertainty about a eucharist presided over by a woman and about ordinations by a woman bishop. Through sympathetic understanding, bishops and dioceses would be open to providing a pastoral alternative for those who dissent. Such conditions, on both sides, would effectively embody the courtesy, respect and differences of principles spoken of by the Lambeth Conference. Understood in this way, we recommend such a proposal be further explored by Provinces in which there is serious dissent.'

From a theological point of view I regard the Act of Synod as a proper exercise in the Church's pastoral 'economy'. I do not apologize for this Orthodox term, which is, after all, related to the word *oikumenē*, ecumenical, and which means something like 'good household management'. There is a long, official, history of Anglican appeal to the principle of 'economy' going back to the 1930 Lambeth Conference, which helpfully gives us a useful working definition: ' "economy" is a technical term representing administrative action to meet a temporary situation without prejudice to any principle of ecclesiastical order'.[20] Temporary here has to be seen in the light of generous Eastern Orthodox time-scales. Parallel ethnic episcopal jurisdictions in the same geographical regions have been around for many centuries among the Orthodox. The practice is still justified by reason of pastoral 'economy', without prejudice to the ecclesiological *norm* of geographical diocesan episcopacy. The parallel here with our own situation is instructive: such parallel episcopal ministries are of course within an acknowledged *single communion*. Similarly with the Roman Catholic Uniate Rites and the Western Latin Rite parallel episcopates: there is no question of their not being in communion with each other. However, in both cases (Roman Catholic and Eastern Orthodox) a shared communion does not imply simple, practical, interchangeability of priests or bishops. Indeed, except in emergencies, the 'rites' or 'jurisdictions' are in no way interchangeable in the sense of priests and bishops presiding in each other's churches sacramentally.

Looked at as an exercise of economy, what is the status of the Act of Synod? An Act of Synod is a solemn synodical act of the Church, falling short of law, either canon law or statute law via a synodical measure. It fits very well into the Lambeth definition of 'economy', 'an administrative action

---

[20] Lambeth Conference, 1930, p. 128, n. 1.

... without prejudice to a principle of ecclesiastical order'. But for a solemn action of the Church the Act of Synod and its detail is not well known. How many parishes and clergy possess a copy, even among those against the ordination of women? I also detect that there are growing numbers of bishops and clergy who have been ordained since the Act of Synod who are very unfamiliar with it. There will also be those who have not gone through the years of debate, conflict and discussion, who perhaps have little patience for its continued provision for dissent. Whether we like the Act of Synod, or whether we want it repealed, while the Act of Synod remains there is need to make its provision known and understood. The Act of Synod will require continued education.

I now move to the Provincial Episcopal Visitors themselves. The first thing to remember about the Provincial Episcopal Visitor is that he comes with the authority of the Metropolitan of the respective Province, through whom the diocesan and suffragan bishops also derive their episcopal orders. Moreover, the PEV takes on certain pastoral and sacramental responsibilities within parishes in a given diocese after petition of the parish concerned to the diocesan, *and the diocesan's invitation*. We are here dealing with *extended* episcopal oversight, rather than parallel *episkopē* in the strict sense. Everything should be done by diocese, parish and PEV to emphasize this. For example, it should be good practice that PEVs are appointed Assistant Bishops in dioceses, thus making it clearer to all concerned that PEVs do not come in 'from the outside' but are part of the diocesan family as well as via the Metropolitan of the Province. Some dioceses also ensure that the PEVs as Assistant Bishops or simply as PEVs are invited to the bishop's staff meeting. Obviously, the PEVs will not be able to go to every staff meeting, but good practice would make them welcome whenever possible. There is a parallel here in that many bishops' staff meetings make special provision for a woman's voice and place (sometimes the Dean of Women's Ministry or equivalent). In a 'process of reception' a diocesan staff meeting should be broad enough to welcome both. Similarly at Institutions the PEV could share the service with the diocesan whose extended authority he will share in the oversight of the parish and priest.

Mutual trust must also condition episcopal relations with parishes. The Act of Synod makes consultation between a parish and the relevant PEV appropriate even before the passing of Resolution C. Sometimes contact between the PEV and such a parish can be construed as the exercise of 'undue influence'. Diocesan staff can be suspicious. Language such as 'building up their own empire' can be heard. A case I am aware of in the Lichfield diocese could have created mutual suspicion and mistrust. So an informal code of practice was developed in which the PEV and the Lichfield bishops exchange their engagement lists so that we all know when we are going to particular churches for services or PCCs. From such trust and mutual consultation derives a wider benefit. In discussing A and B appointments, or even 'no resolution appointments' the PEV often knows of possible clergy, or of pitfalls and skeletons in cupboards in relation to particular names: equally the diocesan staff can help the PEV in a similar way. The PEV can have a wider ministry to many clergy who remain opposed, even if their parishes have not passed a resolution requesting extended episcopal care.

Pastoral sensitivity *also* needs to be demonstrated in relation to the Act of Synod and women priests; the very existence of the Act of Synod and parishes passing resolutions against the ministry of women priests is in one sense an 'affront' to women priests. There is anger that this machinery has to exist. Pain is felt on both sides. We need as the years go by to ensure we do not take this pain for granted or minimize its continuance. Diocesan celebrations of the Eucharist are painful for both sides, whether people are present or absent themselves. At a recent clergy conference clergy 'against' attended for the first time since 'the vote'. Clergy of both convictions planned the worship. A daily 'double' eucharist was provided. Of course in all sorts of ways this was unsatisfactory, but it represented where the Church of England is at the present time in a period of reception. Equally importantly, it meant that people of both convictions met in the Conference and debated and prayed together. A significant number of people managed to attend *both* Eucharists, some communicated at one or the other, others communicated at both! The Maundy Thursday renewal of priestly vows is also a potentially contentious and sensitive issue.[21] So also are Continuing Ministerial Education conferences and other occasions where great sensitivity needs to be exercised as to how a eucharistic presidents' rota is drawn up. It is better to have some agreed format in advance of a meeting when this problem is likely to arise.

What of the future? I would suggest that we resist the temptation to impose a mandatory acceptance of the ordination of women by withdrawing the provisions of the Act of Synod: this would not be true to the theology of reception already referred to and which was the basis of the Lambeth Conference discussion of women's ordination to both the presbyterate and episcopate in 1988; and which was especially commended in the Eames Reports. Equally, I see no need to go further in the direction of a so-called 'Third Province'. Should the Church of England proceed to ordain women to the episcopate, admittedly a new situation would have arisen and we should need to look again at the weight of opposition. But a 'Third Province' is the wrong ecclesial model. Provinces are geographical divisions of the

---

[21] Cf. the paper by the Bishop of Basingstoke for one constructive way forward here.

universal Church, regional groups of dioceses or particular churches. What the Act of Synod provides in its option for PEVs is *not* a territorial-based episcopal ministry but the possibility of a *distinct ecclesial* tradition with its own ethos, discipline and culture. In the Western Church some such cultural provision was commended by the Fourth Lateran Council, Canon 9, where the provision was made for an episcopal vicar in bishop's orders to ensure pastoral care and the sacraments for those of different rites and languages without prejudice to the normal principle of a single bishop for a diocese or city.[22] There are other models to be found elsewhere in Christendom. There are even models in existence elsewhere within the Anglican Communion; such as the Diocese of Aotearoa (New Zealand). This model includes a 'distinct ecclesial' jurisdiction as part of the wider Province from which they derive their authority. But importantly, the diocese is in communion with the wider Church.

I have spoken of trust, respect and, in effect, 'the maintenance of the highest possible degree of communion' (Lambeth Conference 1988, Resolution 1.a). The Act of Synod and Lambeth Conference presupposes that communion is *not* black and white; we are not in communion or out of communion absolutely. There *is* formal ecclesial communion; but where there is no charity this can be less than real. Equally, where there is not yet full ecclesial communion there can be, as Vatican II put it, 'a real though imperfect communion'; as, for example, between the

---

[22] '... *sed si propter praedictas causas urgens necessitas postulaverit, pontifex loci catholicum praesulem, nationibus illis conformem, provida deliberatione constituat sibi vicarium in praedictis, qui ei per omnia sit obediens et subiectus, ...*' Norman P. Tanner (ed.), *Decrees of the Ecumenical Councils*, vol. 1: *Nicaea I to Lateran V* (London: Sheed & Ward, 1990), p. 239.

Church of Rome and the Eastern Orthodox Churches.[23] If it is the case that Rome and the East are in 'real though imperfect communion' and yet there is still the powerful antagonism between Latin Rite and Orthodox in say Russia, then *our* internal antagonism within the Anglican Communion (real and painful as it is) is put in perspective.

Significantly, Pope John Paul II and Archbishop Robert Runcie in their *Common Declaration* of 1989 also used the language of Vatican II in speaking of Anglican–Roman Catholic Relations *after* the ordination of women to the priesthood in a number of Anglican provinces: 'We also urge our clergy and faithful not to neglect or undervalue that certain yet imperfect communion we already share.' If this could be said by Pope and Archbishop of Anglican–Roman Catholic relations in spite of the ordination of women and the traditional non-recognition of Anglican orders by the Roman Catholic Church, Anglicans should be cautious of speaking in too absolute terms about the lack of communion among themselves.[24] Equally, Anglicans need to be honest and realistic that there is a restricted or impaired communion within the Anglican Communion as a result of different practices over the ordination of women to the presbyterate and episcopate. For example, the fact that not only cannot a woman bishop be canonically recognized in the Church of England at the present time but also as a result the men as well as the women ordained by her cannot be recognized or licensed. This is at least a diminished communion compared with the situation in which all bishops and priests were canonically interchangeable.

---

[23] Decree on Ecumenism, 3, '. . . *in quadam cum ecclesia catholica communione, etsi non perfecta, constituuntur*'. Pope Paul VI spoke more than once to the Ecumenical Patriarch in terms of an 'almost perfect communion' as his gloss on Vatican II. Cf. Edward Yarnold, *They are in Earnest* (Slough: St Paul Publications, 1982), p. 99.

[24] Cf. *One in Hope* (London: Church House Publishing and Catholic Truth Society, 1989), p. 8.

But there has never been a complete fullness of communion within the Church. By this I do not only mean the eschatological fullness of communion which God will give in the completion of his Kingdom, for there have always been differences of importance which have eroded or impaired communion in the Church. So Christians have always had the duty to 'maintain the highest possible degree of communion' during times of sharp debate and difference of practice in a period of reception. May Anglicans of different convictions held with integrity continue to attempt to do this until the process of reception is clearer for all, not simply the majority.

7

RECEPTION AND DIVISION IN THE CHURCH

Paul Richardson

Reception has been defined as 'the process through which an ecclesiastical community incorporates into its own life a particular decision, teaching or practice'.[1] Purists have argued that in reception an institution or ecclesial community accepts a doctrine or a tradition that did not originate within itself, but the more general view has been that, while reception must always involve a certain otherness, a distance between the giver and the receiver, it can occur within the sphere of a single church. When this happens, however, the process of reception within a particular ecclesial community takes place against the background of what is happening within the context of the wider Christian Church. Reception is not a purely passive process; it involves discussion and discernment as well as the attempt to see whether what is proposed for reception is appropriate and relevant in the ongoing life of the Church. It involves all members of the Church, both clergy and laity, and calls both for the exercise of critical judgement and for prayerful reflection to determine whether what has been offered for reception can win the consent of believing hearts and minds and so be assimilated into the life of faith. On no account should reception be understood merely as giving people time to come to terms with change, still less as a period of 'softening up' for those who initially appear hostile to a new development. In reception an appeal is

[1] T. Rausch, art. 'Reception', *The New Dictionary of Theology* (Manila, n.d.).

made to the *sensus fidei*, the instinctive, connatural, spon-
taneous sense of faith that is possessed by baptized members
of the body of Christ who are attempting to live the
Christian life in the power of the Spirit. Vatican II actually
taught that the *consensus fidelium* is infallible: 'The body of
the faithful as a whole, anointed as they are by the Holy
One, cannot err in matters of belief' (Dogmatic Constitution on the Church, 12). Many Roman Catholic theologians
are at pains to argue that reception does not validate the
decision of an ecclesial teaching office. It is regarded by
them as a witness by the *consensus fidelium* to a given decision's truth and seviceableness.

The concept of reception is used today in a number of
different areas. In its historical sense, it is used to describe
the process by which local churches accepted the decisions
of councils such as Nicaea and Chalcedon. In ecumenical
usage, the term refers to the acceptance by one church of
decisions or documents of another church. As John
Zizioulas has pointed out, ultimately it means that one
church accepts another church as authentically Christian; it
describes the 'reception of one Church by another Church'.[2]
Within the Anglican Communion the notion of reception
has played a major role in debates about the ordination of
women. In the first instance it was argued that Anglicans
were entitled to take this step in the hope that eventually it
would be received by other ecumenical partners such as the
Roman Catholic Church and the Orthodox who at present
reject it. After the ordination of women had been accepted,
many Anglicans then appealed to the concept of reception
to justify their readiness to permit people who dissented
from the new development to remain in the Church and to
hold office in it. The argument that the Church is at present
in the midst of a process of reception as far as the ordination

---

[2] J. Zizioulas, 'The Theological Problem of Reception', *One in Christ* 3 (1985): 189.

of women is concerned and that during this period those on different sides in the debate should maintain 'the highest possible degree of communion in spite of difference' is a major theme in the report of the Eames Commission.[3] The final report of the Commission also maintained that 'because we are part of the One, Holy, Catholic, and Apostolic Church, reception is never a matter for each tradition in isolation'.[4]

Reception has been traced back to the New Testament. Paul points out to the Corinthians that they have 'received' the gospel he preached (1 Corinthians 12.1). We need to beware of interpreting Paul's own reception of the gospel in a purely individual sense. Certainly his experience on the road to Damascus was important to him, but Acts 9.19–20 tells us that he spent an unknown number of days with the disciples in the city before he began to proclaim the gospel. John Zizioulas has reminded us that the Church was born out of a process of reception, a process he rightly describes as twofold. In the New Testament account, the Church receives the gospel, the love of God incarnate in his Son, Jesus Christ, conveyed to her in the power of the Spirit. But she must also be prepared to receive from the world with which she is called to remain in constant dialogue. In a penetrating comment, Zizioulas claims that 'what we used to call "mission" is better rendered with notions and nuances of reception because "mission" is loaded with ideas of aggressiveness whereas the Church should be *offering herself to the world for reception* instead of *imposing* herself on it'.[5]

Although the concept of reception is both rich and useful, it is not without its problems. In 1972 Yves Congar

---

[3] *The Eames Commission, Official Reports* (Toronto: Anglican Book Centre, 1994), p. 85.
[4] Ibid.
[5] Zizioulas, 'Theological Problem', p. 189 (italics original).

described it as a theme 'that is not often examined'.[6] Many commentators argue that it was significant in the Early Church but passed out of use when a hierarchical model of the Church that emphasized obedience became more important in the Middle Ages, although it is conceded that Orthodoxy has always stressed the importance of reception as an indication that a council was truly ecumenical. It is seen as deriving from a theology of communion that emphasises the importance of local churches and of the guiding presence of the Holy Spirit. Theologians associated with this approach, like Yves Congar and J.M.R. Tillard, are the ones who have emphasized reception. Yet even in the case of the early councils of the Church, there is often a lack of clarity about what reception actually involved. Those present at ecumenical councils did not think of themselves as proposing doctrines for reception by the universal Church. They believed that they were authorized to serve as representatives of the whole Church to proclaim a valid interpretation of Scripture and tradition that would be binding on the whole Church. However, the authority and ecumenicity of councils appears not to have been determined by who was present but by what a foremost scholar of the period has termed a *consensio antiquitatis et universitatis* (a consensus with antiquity and the universal church).[7] Councils set out to determine what the Church already believed and taught. It was the reception of the decisions of a council by the local churches that determined whether the council had in fact preserved the faith of antiquity. The process could take a good deal of time and often a key moment in the reception of a council was the acceptance of its teaching at a subsequent council. Some

[6] Y. Congar, 'Reception as an Ecclesiological Reality' in G. Alberigo and A. Weiler (eds.), *Election and Consensus in the Church* (New York): Herder and Herder 1972), p. 43.

[7] Herman Josef Sieben, quoted by R.R. Gaillardetz, *Teaching with Authority* (Collegeville: Liturgical Press, 1997), p. 196.

councils, like the 'robbers council of Ephesus' failed to be received and are not counted as ecumenical councils. But even in the case of ecumenical councils like Nicaea and Chalcedon there were considerable numbers of Christians who rejected them and who continue to reject them even today.

This raises the question of whether a doctrine or the decision of a council can ever be said to be finally received. Sometimes a development appears to have been received only to be rejected later and then possibly 're-received'! This happened in the case of private confession. The custom seems to have begun among Irish monks and then to have spread to the rest of the Church. It was made binding on the faithful at least once a year by the Lateran Council in 1215 only to be challenged at the Reformation. Yves Congar once expressed the view that we need a re-reception by the churches of a number of the normative creeds and theological traditions that govern their lives and were drawn up by those churches in isolation. He instanced *Pastor aeternus*, the Augsburg Confession and Palamism as examples of what he had in mind.[8]

On the other hand the canon of the New Testament is a good example of a decision that does appear to have been finally received by the Church even if there are some scholars today who would like us to give serious attention to the so-called 'apocryphal Gospels'. In the very Early Church there was no agreed canon of the New Testament. Works such as the *Shepherd of Hermas*, the *Epistle of Barnabas*, and the *Didache* can be found listed as canonical works. The Muratorian fragment includes as canonical the *Apocalypse of Peter*. In time, however, an agreed canon did come to be widely accepted. Faced by the departures from the faith held by the *sensus fidelium*, the Church was led to recognize the authority of those books that reflected and witnessed to that faith.

[8] Y. Congar, *Diversity and Communion* (London: SCM Press, 1984), p. 171.

Cardinal Willebrands has warned that we should not judge reception by counting heads. 'Is reception a sociological process? Can it be understood in a purely numerical or quantitative manner, that is to say, in the sense of statistical majority or convictions?' he asks. But then he goes on to remark: 'We are surely agreed that one cannot speak of true reception in a case where only a faithful few accept and confirm the result of dialogue.'[9] At the Second Council of Nicaea (753) three criteria were laid down for deciding whether a council was truly ecumenical. Decisions must be received by the whole Church; they must be in agreement with previous ecumenical councils; and there must be participation, either personal or through representation, by the five patriarchal sees and in particular by the See of Rome.[10] The Orthodox theologian John Zizioulas has argued that we do need a ministry of universal reception and that this can only be exercised by the Bishop of Rome.[11]

This raises the question of authority in the Church and of different levels of reception, an idea common among Roman Catholic theologians. Should we distinguish between the 'diffuse reception' of the faithful, the reception by theologians, and the crucial role played by bishops and by the bishop of Rome in particular? A key factor for Roman Catholics is the place of the magisterium. Vatican I famously asserted that papal definitions are 'irreformable of themselves and not from the consent of the Church' (Denzinger-Schonmetzer 3074). Commentators are divided about what this means, but the majority is of the opinion that it was intended to rule out Gallican attempts to appeal

[9] J. Willebrands, 'The Ecumenical Dialogue and its Reception', *One in Christ* 3 (1985), p. 22.

[10] Gaillardetz, *Teaching with Authority*, p. 195.

[11] Zizioulas, 'Theological Problem', p. 187.

from papal decisions to the episcopate as a whole. It does not mean that papal pronouncements can be made apart from the faith of the Church. When he speaks infallibly, the Pope is meant to reflect the *consensus fidelium*, the common mind of the faithful around the world. Owen Chadwick has described how Fessler, the German secretary of the council, wrote a book to make this point just after the council was concluded and that Pope Pius IX gave explicit approval to his interpretation.[12] According to Francis Sullivan, SJ, while reception does not demonstrate the truth of an infallible pronouncement by the Pope, we should expect to see such a statement received by the faithful as an indication that the conditions for an infallible pronouncement have been met. He quotes Karl Rahner to the effect that 'it follows, of course, although Vatican II does not say so, that if a definition in the end failed to enjoy such a reception on the part of the Church, this would prove that the definition had not in fact met the stringent requirements for an *ex cathedra* pronouncement'.[13]

To see how reception functions in Catholic theology, it is necessary to understand what is meant by the process. Ecumenical theologians have commonly stressed that in the reception of a document coming from another church, we have to ask ourselves whether we see in it the faith of the universal Church as we have understood it. What is called for is an act of discernment. Catholic theologians have also spoken in these terms when referring to reception in an ecumenical context, but in talking about the reception of the decisions of the magisterium they have sometimes adopted a slightly different approach. In these circumstances the questions they have suggested for consideration

---

[12] O. Chadwick, *A History of the Papacy 1830–1914* (Oxford: Clarendon Press, 1997), p. 221.
[13] F. Sullivan, *Magisterium: Teaching Authority in the Catholic Church* (New York: Paulist Press, 1983), pp. 108–9.

have been more concerned with the relevance and appropriateness of a papal document or decision than about whether it reflects the faith of the Church. Yves Congar has emphasized that reception 'does not confer validity, but affirms, acknowledges and attests that this matter is for the good of the Church'.[14] J.M.R. Tillard has argued that reception is the 'response of a group, grounded in a judgement as to whether what is proposed is really in tune with the mind, the real needs, the common good of this group'.[15] This is why reception is not a matter for individuals but for the Christian community. Tillard goes so far as to claim that a proposition may be true and in harmony with Christian doctrine but still not be received because it is not what the People of God need here and now. Pope John XXIII's attempt to promote the use of Latin in the Catholic Church would be an example of a papal initiative not received in this sense.

The understanding of reception as a process to test the relevance and appropriateness of church teaching has sometimes been used in the Roman Catholic Church to avoid awkward questions of truth in the controversy over birth control. Richard Gaillardetz is a Catholic theologian who is bold enough to try to find a way through this particular minefield. He suggests the fact that *Humanae vitae* has not been received by the faithful does not mean it is false. It has not been rejected, only ignored. It is perceived as irrelevant, lacking in 'transformative power' and therefore would be best forgotten.[16] Here is a 'third way' that both saves face for the magisterium and still frees the faithful from the obligation to a burdensome rule. Unfortunately it also sounds like special pleading. The *consensus fidelium* has

---

[14] Rausch, 'Reception', p. 829.
[15] J.M.R. Tillard, 'Did We "Receive" Vatican II?', *One in Christ* 4 (1985): 276.
[16] Gaillardetz, *Teaching with Authority*, p. 235.

surely not just ignored papal teaching as irrelevant; it has examined the logic behind it and rejected it.

The questions 'Does this really state the faith? Is it in accord with the apostolic and catholic faith as we have received it?' are of pivotal importance in the process of reception. Questions of relevance and appropriateness are also useful, but they cannot be discussed in isolation from questions about truth and faithfulness to Scripture and tradition. The issue of relevance can be of key significance where the Church is seeking to promote inculturation and striving to articulate an understanding of the gospel that is faithful to tradition but also speaks to the contemporary situation. But local initiatives cannot be pursued in isolation. There must be a dialogue across cultures, both to enable the universal Church to learn from what is happening in different parts of the world and also to assist in the process of discernment.

The process of reception has become more complex in the global Church. One of the features of the 1998 Lambeth Conference was the inability of some bishops from Western nations to recognize the need for dialogue with bishops and theologians from the South. There was a reluctance to recognize that fresh perspectives yield new insights into the meaning of the biblical text. Critical scholarship of the 1960s still has its place but it is not the only key to unlock the meaning of the scriptures. The gospel discloses unsuspected aspects of its truth, unexplored depths of meaning, as it comes into contact with different world-views and is brought into dialogue with new cultures and philosophies. Fresh insights generated by this process then need to be received by the Church as a whole to prevent one part of the Church being trapped by its own perspective or being blinded by its own culture. None of this is really new. Tradition has always developed as the gospel has come into dialogue with new world-views and Christians have continued to pray, worship, witness and reflect on their faith.

In some cases what was considered orthodoxy in the early years of the Church had come to be regarded as heresy in later centuries because of the dynamic movement of Tradition. Doctrines had to be received and re-received by the Church. There is continuity but also growth and development. In a global Church we are challenged to hold together universal coherence and genuine inculturation in a fruitful relationship. Somehow we must foster a global vision to prevent the local church becoming culture-bound and yet at the same time allow the Church to enter into dialogue with the local culture to prevent it seeming foreign and irrelevant.

What light does this discussion shed on debates in contemporary Anglicanism? In the first place, I think we should be wary of 'provincial autonomy'. Each part of the Church needs to be open to the wider whole. Anglicans in one part of the Church should remain in dialogue with Anglicans elsewhere in the world, otherwise the Anglican Communion will fragment and fall apart. In the present ecumenical context, we need to be ready to listen to what other churches are saying. Many Anglicans hope that Roman Catholics will eventually receive the ordination of women, and even those of us who do not necessarily share this hope can regret that, by ruling out all discussion of the subject, Pope John Paul II has made it difficult for loyal members of his church to give careful consideration to a development that has taken place in what Anglicans at least would regard as a 'sister church'. But by the same token, it was unfortunate that the General Synod of the Church of England could declare back in the early 1970s that there were not serious theological objections to the ordination of women when Roman Catholic theologians of the stature of Hans urs von Balthasar and Louis Bouyer have found a number of such objections. Anglicans of all persuasions have a duty to give careful attention to the teaching of the Roman Catholic Church as expressed in such documents as

Inter insigniories, Mulieris dignitatem or *Ordinatio sacerdotalis* just as Roman Catholics have an ecumenical responsibility to weigh careful what is happening in the Anglican Communion.

Second, I think we should be wary of making use of the concept of reception to license just any experimental development in the Church. The question of when it is right to propose a development for reception is a sensitive and difficult one. A church taking such a step should be able to appeal to justification in scripture and tradition and to the widespread consent among the faithful before it goes ahead. Under a system of synodical government there is danger that pressure groups will use their voting power to force a church to adopt a policy for which there is little justification in Scripture and tradition and then go on to argue that it is right to present the innovation as a matter for reception by the whole Church. It is unlikely that such an innovation will be accepted, but the process of reception could turn out to be quite disastrous for the Church that had authorized the development. Henry Chadwick has issued a warning that deserves careful notice:

> It is a safe generalisation that there is friction in the Church when someone wishes to modify or even discard one of the three norms that evolved in the second century. The continuing Church on earth needs to affirm its faith, needs to acknowledge the witness of scripture, needs to admit to its community by baptism in the name of Christ, and, in obedience to his command to renew its life by the eucharistic memorial. Moreover, for the sake of its own coherence, it needs a ministry generally accepted as possessing a commission given by Christ in his Church, to serve and to safeguard the word and sacraments. In these areas of Bible, Creed, Sacraments and Ministry, the Church understands herself to have received divine gifts (as in Ephesians 4), *dona donata*, touching the deepest roots of Christian existence, and therefore needing to be handled with sensitivity.[17]

[17] H. Chadwick, *Tradition and Exploration: Collected Papers on Theology and the Church* (Norwich: Canterbury Press, 1994), p. 17.

Third, reception is not a process that can be rushed. Once the Church has allowed a particular development to take place, it may take many years before a consensus is formed and the decision is truly received. We need to be aware of the danger of ascribing absolute power to the General Synod of the Church of England to determine doctrinal development in the Church just at the time when Roman Catholic theologians are trying to stress that the papacy must be sensitive to the *consensus fidelium*.

Gillian Evans has stressed the distinction between reception and tolerance. Toleration need not imply dialogue, discussion, co-operation in a shared process of discernment. As Gillian Evans expresses it, 'toleration sits uneasily with reception because it allows the other to continue in his or her opinion with real acceptance of the view tolerated, without moving position, without seriously considering whether it might be possible that the two views are one'.[18] She goes on to identify two mindsets which she sees as hostile to reception. The first she terms 'churchmanship' when Christians start to 'identify themselves first and foremost as (for example) "Baptist" or "Orthodox" or "Anglican" or even as "Southern Baptist", "Russian Orthodox" or "High Anglican" rather than as Christians'.[19] The second she labels a 'cultural mindset' where Christians living in one particular culture feel they cannot receive documents or statements from Christians living in a different part of the world. The eventual result of this way of thinking, she rightly argues, would be a collection of bodies calling themselves churches that had no connection with each other.

Gillian Evans is right to warn of the inadequacy of toleration, but she ignores what postmodernist critics see as the great danger inherent in the liberal approach to issues of

[18] G.R. Evans, *The Reception of the Faith* (London: SPCK, 1997), p. 155.
[19] Evans, *Reception of the Faith*, p. 174.

cultural and philosophical diversity: the push for assimilation. As Zygmunt Bauman has argued, those who accept assimilation into liberal society in effect surrender their own culture and values.[20] We must not expect that the process of reception will end in complete victory for one side or the other. This will be hard for those who consider themselves to be on the side of progress and enlightenment to accept. Reception is meant to be a communal process. As it takes place, different sides in debates that divide the Church come to see that their conflicting perspectives can often each witness to an aspect of the truth that somehow transcends all of them. In such a situation, it does no good to describe one side in a debate as 'beached whales' or 'dinosaurs' or to attempt to marginalize them in the life of the Church. At the very least, reception surely involves our accepting those with whom we disagree, honouring the sincerity of their commitment as Christians and their integrity as theologians. The Australian theologian Winifred Wing Han Lamb has drawn on the work of the educationalist R.K. Elliott to describe the way in which she thinks inter-faith dialogue should take place.[21] Her remarks are relevant to understanding the process of reception within the Church. Elliott stresses the importance of friendship and calls for what he calls 'double-minded thinkers' who do not try to be neutral and who do not underestimate their differences with people who hold other views but who nonetheless try to understand an apparently opposing position sympathetically, from the inside. If we take other people's views seriously, it may not convert us to their opinions but it can still enlarge our understanding of the Christian faith and lead us to a fresh appreciation of the

[20] Z. Bauman, *Modernity and Ambivalence* (Oxford: Polity Press, 1991).

[21] Winifred Wing Han Lamb, ' "The Open Heaven": Understanding Other Faiths in God's World', in V. Pfitzner and H. Regan (eds), *The Task of Theology Today* (Edinburgh: T&T Clark, 1999), pp. 163–91.

position we ourselves hold. When the debate about the ordination of women finally comes to a close (if it ever does) I am convinced that all sides in the dispute that has divided the Church of England will be seen to have made a contribution and to have helped the Church to come to deeper understanding, a further reception, of the revelation given to us in Christ. Proponents of the ordination of women have reminded us of the need for the Church to be inclusive and of the gifts that women can bring to the ministry of the Church. Opponents have reminded us of our place in the wider Church, of our need to be attentive to tradition and to the *consensus fidelium*.

The Catholic priest and sociologist Andrew Greeley has called for an understanding of authority as 'inviting, calling and attracting' rather than as 'controlling directing and regulating'. He has argued that such a model is more appropriate for the present time when authoritative control is under threat everywhere and people dislike being forced to act by sanctions or force. He has appealed for the Church to pattern its use of authority to reflect God as final cause rather than God as efficient cause. God lures us, attracts us, moves us by his divine beauty to seek after him and answer his call. In Greeley's words, 'there must be a reform – at every level of authority in the Church – in which authority moves more in the direction of charm, of final cause, of the beauty of the incredibly attractive God, of a God who calls, even a God who tries to lure us with beauty'.[22] As Greeley makes clear, this does not mean there is no need for basic book-keeping and house-keeping rules or for disciplinary canons. What he is talking about is the manner in which the Church teaches doctrine and attempts to set forth the truth about God. Essentially the model he describes fits very well with an understanding of the importance of reception. Although Greeley is reacting against a hier-

[22] A.M. Greeley, 'Authority as Charm', *America*, 20 November 1999.

archical model of the Church where all major decisions are reserved to the magisterium, what he has to say applies just as much to a synodical church in which political lobbies and pressure groups exercise the major power to influence change.

Greeley provides an attractive model of decision-making that fits in well with the doctrine of reception. Unfortunately, and surprisingly for a sociologist, he fails to look at the context in which decisions are made in the Church today. The post-liberal Lutheran theologian George Lindbeck has sounded a warning about the way in which Christian thinking at the present time is no longer shaped by reading and reflecting on Scripture. As he sees it, the *sensus fidelium* needs to be nourished by Scripture transmitted through liturgy, preaching, catechesis, and personal reading. Today, he feels, the Bible is a closed book even to many church members. At a time when theology is pluralistic, and when institutions like churches are under pressure to change and adapt, and tradition is everywhere facing attack, he sees a weakening of a sense of community in the Church. Instead of seeing the Bible as a narrative that tells the story of God's dealings with the human race, scholars concentrate on providing diverse and tentative historical reconstructions of the biblical message. The result is a weakening of the *sensus fidelium* to which appeal must be made to settle disputes in the Church just at a time when the Christian community is facing divisions caused by the rapid pace of change.[23] Lindbeck's analysis could be extended by pointing out the extent to which thinking in the Church is influenced by secular pressures and movements, often given a big boost by the mass media. The Church certainly needs to read the signs of the times, but

---

[23] G. Lindbeck, 'Scripture, Consensus and Community', in *Biblical Interpretation in Crisis: The Ratzinger Conference on Bible and Church*, ed. Richard John Neuhaus (Grand Rapids: Eerdmans, 1989).

this surely does not mean jumping on every passing bandwagon or embracing every passing trend. The gospel needs to relate to secular culture, but Christians are asked to transform the world not to conform to it. We can certainly learn from movements like Marxism or feminism but this does not mean embracing their every dogma or putting them above criticism. The doctrine of reception still has a lot to offer the Church, but Lindbeck and others are right to warn us of the ambiguous context in which the process of reception takes place in the Church of today.

8

LEARNING TO LIVE WITH DIFFERENCE

Geoffrey Rowell

On the feast of St Martin, 11 November 1992, the General Synod of the Church of England agreed, by the slimmest of majorities, that women should be permitted to be ordained to the priesthood. The slim majority was, admittedly, in the context of the requirement for a two-thirds majority in each of the three houses of the synod (bishops, clergy and laity), for this was rightly deemed to be a matter touching the faith and order of the Church. It is worth noting, however, that the two-thirds requirement was itself a reduction from the three-quarters that had been the original requirement for such measures; and that had a two-thirds requirement been in force at an earlier date the scheme for Anglican–Methodist unity would have been approved. For many the slim vote in favour came at the end of a long and arduous campaign, a struggle for justice and equality, for the proper recognition of the gifts that women ordained to the priesthood would bring to the ministry of the Church. The scenes of celebration outside Church House Westminster that evening testified to the sense of victory that was shared by many. For others, however, this was a bitter – for some devastating – blow to their understanding of the nature of the Church, and in particular to the nature of the Church of England as 'part of the one, holy, catholic and apostolic Church'. The ancient story of St Martin cutting his cloak in two to clothe a beggar seemed to have gained a new reference to the rending of a seamless garment.

What is the consequence of that vote in the General Synod for those of us who continue to live, minister and worship in the Church of England? It is a church that has chosen to allow those of differing viewpoints on the question of the ordination of women to the priesthood to remain in one church, a church in which those not persuaded of the rightness of the 1992 vote (and in that number I include myself) were to be full and honoured members: continuing 'to hold a legitimate and recognized position within the Church of England' (as *Bonds of Peace* puts it). Resolution III.4 of the 1998 Lambeth Conference (on the Eames Commission reports on women bishops) was clearly debated with the sense that those who accept the ordination of women to the priesthood and episcopate and those who dissent from that ordination are equally loyal Anglicans.

My reflections are at once theological and practical and pastoral. A bishop must be all of those things. There must be a theological basis for any position taken. It cannot simply be a matter of prejudice, or sociology, or psychology: though all need to recognize that all those things undoubtedly influence and shape all our theological discussion. Furthermore, bishops are faced not just with theoretical and abstract statements of theology, but with their practical working-out in the life of the Church at all levels. Again, a bishop must be sensitive to the fact that he is called to be the pastor of the *whole* people of God, and, in this instance, that he is called to minister to those with differing viewpoints on the question of women priests, and to the women ordained to the priesthood for whom he has episcopal responsibility.

First let me sketch some necessary background and some ecclesiological reflections. There is undoubtedly a sociological and cultural dimension to the movement that, for the Church of England, culminated in the 1992 vote. Questions of the participation of women in the ministry of churches across the whole spectrum of Christian tradition are by and large modern, Western, questions. There were women who preached in some of the radical seventeenth-century sects. There were women who exercised a powerful ministry among the Quakers, though they were not ministers because Quakers have no ordained ministry. There were some women who were recognized as ministers among the Bible Christians and Primitive Methodists. Nevertheless, at the end of the last century there was strong resistance to women being admitted as full members of the Methodist Conference. Even were they to be admitted, said Hugh Price Hughes, one of their most prominent divines, who thought they should not, they would have no significant role, and they would merely be 'like poppies in a cornfield'. Chauvinism there certainly was, but even among denominations that did not claim an ordained *priesthood* the question of the ordination of women did not come significantly to the fore until the 1960s. It is largely a recent issue. The two largest bodies of Christians (the Roman Catholic and Orthodox Churches), despite some movement in favour of women priests (much more in the former than in the latter), stand by the continuous tradition of a male priesthood. Anglicans have historically claimed to stand on Scripture and 'the ancient common traditions' (a phrase notably used by Archbishop Michael Ramsey and Pope Paul VI in the joint communiqué after their March 1966 meeting in Rome). It was Scripture and the ancient common traditions that were normative for both faith and order, and Anglicans were required to receive nothing as of faith save what Holy Scripture and the ancient common traditions required. This was and is a fundamental Christian liberty for Anglicans. It has also been one of the significant planks of Anglican apologetic against the Church of Rome that Rome has, as matters of faith, required acceptance of doctrines and practices that have no sure grounding in Scripture or tradition.

Christianity is a revealed religion. It is that which is received and handed on, and, as Archbishop Bramhall argued in the seventeenth century, that which is handed on consists partly in *credenda* (things meet to be believed) and partly in *agenda* (things meet to be done), among which would be included patterns of liturgy and order. I would argue that for the ordination of women to the priesthood (an admitted innovation) to be received with the assurance of faith that is needed, five things have to be in place. First, it must be clearly shown to be grounded in Scripture, and required by Scripture. Second, it must likewise be shown to be clearly grounded in the tradition of the Church. Third, where such clear grounding cannot be shown, there must be a fully worked-out theology of development accepted by all that can take the weight of demonstrating that this is indeed a legitimate development of both Scripture and tradition (for, as Newman quite rightly pointed out, change does not necessarily equal development: there may be corruption as well as development, and development of doctrine must be measured by some kind of appeal to notes or tests). Fourth, as well as a theology of *development* there must be an acceptance of a developing *authority*: that is, what is the *magisterium* (teaching authority) to which any particular church aspires and how is that magisterium related to the magisterium claimed by other churches. Finally, if the argument thus set forward is sustained, is it then possible to conclude that this development carries with it the sacramental assurance identical with that of the male priesthood of the ordained ministry as received and practised up to this point? As Professor Henry Chadwick commented in the course of the debate about the ordination of women to the priesthood, 'dubious orders are the very devil and Rome stays well clear of them'. (I myself wrote in an article a few years before the 1992 vote that the one sure and certain result of such a vote would be that there would no longer be a commonly accepted ministry in the Church of England.)

Dubious orders are, alas, what we have, and from an Anglican perspective. Moreover, I do not myself see how such a consequence could have been avoided as long as there was a willingness to press ahead by means of a vote in a synod that implicitly claimed to be able to vary the accepted practice of the Church catholic. That was a point made forcefully by the Pope in his annual address to the curia and the Vatican diplomatic corps at the end of 1988. That year, he said, had been marked for him by two sadnesses: the Lefebvrist schism in the Roman Catholic Church, and the failure of the 1988 Lambeth Conference to ask for restraint in the Anglican Communion in the matter of the consecration of women bishops. The ordination of women to the priesthood was, he said, something that not even he had authority to do, as he was bound – as Anglicans have traditionally held themselves to be bound – by Scripture and tradition. (Indeed, there has been a certain irony in Roman Catholic and Orthodox apologists taking the stance of traditional Anglican apologetic in relation to this matter.)

Before the synod's 1992 vote there was, of course, much consultation on both sides of the argument about how to put before the Church of England the consequences of voting one way or another on the issue. I think it may be appropriate, now that some time has passed, to set out a statement that I drew up in consultation with bishops who were troubled by the consequences of the synod approving the ordination of women to the priesthood. I was personally disappointed when the bishops who approved it decided in the end not to issue it. Their grounds were pastoral, which I appreciate now that I myself have episcopal responsibility. They had called their dioceses to prayer and to unity, and for some that meant that issuing a statement on one side ran counter to that genuine pastoral instinct to care for the whole people of God. I still think it would have been more honest and helpful if that statement had been issued (either Michaelmas Day or All Saints' Day had been thought appropriate). Given that bishops who supported the ordination of women to the priesthood, and had also called their dioceses to prayer and unity, did not forbear from issuing statements in a different direction, I think it would have made clear the grounds and character of those concerned to maintain the tradition that the Church had followed since the earliest centuries. This is how the statement read:

(1) Even after so long and protracted a debate it is evident that the Church is deeply divided. We may regret that it has taken up so much of the Church's time and energy, but that it has is an indication that for many it touches the heart of the Church's being, its apostolic faith, order and ministry.

(2) Although the Church necessarily exists in a world of change and flux, it is called above all to a faithfulness to the gospel. As bishops we are called to guard the faith and be obedient to the constraints of unity, for which the Lord prayed on the eve of his Passion.

(3) We are faced with a divisive issue and a disputed question. We do not believe it to be right to proceed to enact legislation that will in practice make such a disputed question a test of Anglican orthodoxy, or a means of introducing doubt into the very heart of the Church's sacramental life.

(4) We are conscious of the continual pleas from the great churches of East and West that unilateral action in this matter by Anglicans runs counter to the growing realization of the unity that Christ wills. This legislation divides and will divide our Church. It also erects new barriers between Anglicans and Roman Catholics and Orthodox, contrary to that growing into unity which is Christ's will.

(5) As bishops in the Catholic tradition we acknowledge the part played by the Catholic revival of the last century in many aspects of women's ministry, notably the religious orders. We pledge ourselves to enable and support the full exercise of women's ministry in the Church of our day, in the diaconate, in the religious orders, and in other ministries, by ensuring that there are adequate opportunities for the fulfilment of ministry in positions of responsibility.

(6) In a Church so deeply divided on this disputed issue, we

cannot think it right to enact legislation, which would in effect unchurch a significant percentage of clergy and laity who are conscientiously opposed to this legislation. We cannot vote to divide. We cannot make what is doubtful into a doctrine requiring universal acceptance.

Two weeks after the vote in the General Synod I preached at All Saints Margaret Street; it was the feast of Christ the King. I thought it right to take as my text the words that John Keble took as his text for the Assize Sermon that marked the beginning of the Oxford Movement in July 1833: 'As for me, God forbid that I should sin against the Lord in ceasing to pray for you; but I will teach you the good and right way.' (1 Samuel 12.23). Keble believed in 1833 that the Church of England was faced with a question of identity. 'On what ground do you stand, O presbyter of the Church of England?' He recalled the Church to the apostolic basis of its faith and the apostolic succession of its episcopal order. In the vote of 1992 the Church of England, through its constitutional organs of government, agreed to enact legislation that needs a doctrine of development to undergird it. I said in that sermon: 'When the Church of England takes this step it is doing two things: it is acting in a Protestant way – the local church has authority to act – but it is applying Roman Catholic arguments about the development of doctrine.' I went on to ask that 'every support must be given to those bishops who are rightly asking that those whose theological convictions about the nature of the Church and its ministry are those to which the Church of England has historically been committed are assured of a *permanent and protected place within the Church*'. Speaking from both 'a theological conviction and a grief observed' I urged that 'those afforded such a [permanent and protected] place are committed not to a sectarian ghetto with boundaries marked by a negative theology, but to living out in the fullest possible way they can the sacramental life of the Church'.

What followed at the beginning of 1993 was a meeting of the House of Bishops in Manchester that produced the document *Bonds of Peace*, which led eventually to the Episcopal Ministry Act of Synod 1993. An act of synod corresponds to an act of convocation, but in relation to the Church of England as a whole. Such acts possess 'great moral force as the considered judgement of the highest and ancient synod of the Province' (see *Bland* v. *Archdeacon of Cheltenham* (1972) ER1012, 1018). That Episcopal Ministry Act established, among other things, the provincial episcopal visitors to minister to and act as ombudsmen for those remaining in the Church of England but unable to give full assent to the validity of the orders of women ordained to the priesthood. The simple reason for withholding that consent is that no individual Christian, no priest, no bishop, no provincial synod can bestow the catholic consent for which the consent of the universal Church is required.

The 1993 Act was devised to deal pastorally with a situation in which there was no longer a commonly accepted ministry within the Church of England. Its concern is with the enacting of 'bonds of peace' (from Paul's 'make fast with the bonds of peace the unity which the Spirit gives': Ephesians 4.3). It recognizes that a situation has been created in which *episkopē* is exercised by bishops who have voted (in good conscience) to enact sacramentally what is at variance with the common tradition, and which calls into question the claim to share in the historic, apostolic ministry of the Church. A vote for variance has inevitably some effect on this traditional Anglican claim — that the orders of the Church of England are those of the whole Church of God. The Episcopal Ministry Act recognizes that belief in the ordination of women to the priesthood is not an article by which the Church stands or falls, and that it is therefore possible to hold with theological integrity, on the one hand, a position which accepts the ordination of women to the priesthood and, on the other, a position which stands by the *status quo ante*. Because that second position was the position of historic Christendom for almost two thousand years it would be difficult to maintain with integrity that such a position did not possess theological integrity. By the Episcopal Ministry Act, the synod therefore endeavoured to find a solution to the divisive situation that had been created by a pastoral provision for episcopal oversight, first at a diocesan level, then at a regional level, and finally at a provincial level.

What kind of understanding lies behind such pastoral provision? At one level it is a recognition that those who find their ecclesiology damaged by the 1992 vote of variance from traditional order, need to have bishops of their integrity (theological persuasion) to whom they can relate. It is a recognition of a very human need. It is also a theological expression of the need to affirm that theological position. It is an outworking of a theology that says: this matter (the ordination of women to the priesthood) is not an article by which the Church stands or falls. It may in the eyes of some, damage the Church of England's claim to catholicity; it may in the eyes of others enhance that claim, where catholicity is understood as inclusiveness at every level of ministry.

A bishop stands as a focus for unity; yet in the circumstances that the 1992 vote brought about, no bishop of either integrity can unequivocally be the focus of unity. A bishop who, like myself, concedes that legally and canonically women have been ordained to the priesthood (for that is a matter of legal fact), but has reservation about the validity of their theological standing as priests in the catholic *oikoumenē* (for they lack catholic consent) is clearly impaired in his ability to act as a focus of unity for the women priests in his diocese or area, and, arguably, for those male clergy (and laity) for whom such a stance is a theological affront. In the same way, a bishop who has ordained women to the priesthood has, for those who hold a 'traditionalist' view, brought about impaired communion in the collegiality of the clergy of his diocese. A woman bishop, about whom the same doubts are held, also draws those whom she ordains, be they male or female, into that same impairment: an impairment that women in the episcopate inevitably magnify. We have been used to saying ecumenically that in a divided Church all the notes of the Church are impaired. What we now have is that impairment brought home within the Church of England. It is not simply a matter of different theological standpoints, but of difference sacramentally enacted. When John Wesley proceeded to ordain ministers, by that action he created a sharpness of division between the Methodist movement and the Church of England that has lasted until this day. Sacramental actions in divisive situations are likely to create – and frequently institutionalize – division.

As a bishop of 'traditionalist' convictions I am quite clear that in this anomalous and divisive situation *how* pastoral care is exercised is as important as *that* it is exercised. The basic truth for all of us is our baptism, our life in Christ, and the call to holiness. That is what is fundamental: not a sociological hermeneutic or a concern for the promotion of egalitarianism over hierarchy. All Christians are under judgement; all churches are under judgement; and therefore all who exercise oversight in churches are under judgement. What we are called to is holiness, likeness to Christ, and to the new life of resurrection. The question for all of us is how can we live in a situation of deep conviction and conscientious division over something that goes to the heart of the Church's sacramental life. And that of course is to speak not just of the Church of England or the Anglican Communion, but of the broken and impaired communion of all Christians. We would do well to attend more to the fundamental imperative of baptism than to the particular calling of ordination, and to look more to the communion we receive and for whose fulfilment we long than to the erection of further barriers of division. The Episcopal Ministry Act of Synod at its best does indeed enable us to strive to 'make fast with the bonds of peace the unity that the Spirit gives'.

The Church of England has endeavoured to find a way of living with division, and a division over something as fundamental to any church's identity as the structure of its ministry, with the impact that has on its sacramental life. It is an admittedly untidy ecclesiology, but that very untidiness, and that very weakness, may have something important to say from a Christian perspective. It was on the eve of my consecration as a bishop – as a bishop in the Church of God, but also a bishop in this untidy situation which I would not have wished to have come about – that an Orthodox priest said to me, 'The Church of England now has the opportunity to show the rest of Christendom how to live with division.' I have valued that encouragement, just as I valued the comment of a Roman Catholic friend who said at the same time, 'You are going to be a bishop in a church that is rather battered, but then I think being battered is being rather like Christ.'

Sooner or later the Church of England will have to face the question of women bishops. There were eleven women bishops from the Anglican Communion at the 1998 Lambeth Conference. I have some sympathy with those who argue that the bishop is the fundamental order of ministry, and that therefore the Church of England ought to have voted (as the Church of Ireland did) to admit women into all three orders of ministry. However, there is also wisdom in a gradualism, and wisdom in the fact that time is needed for a reception of a new doctrine, or a new practice. In other parts of the Anglican Communion where women have been ordained to the priesthood, but particularly in the United States and Canada, there is a sense that 'reception' has been completed, and that all that remains is for the few recalcitrants to be brought into line. It was out of concern for those 'recalcitrants' in the Episcopal Church of the United States of America who felt themselves to be in danger of being forced out of the Church to which they belonged, as well as because dialogue is itself important, that I initiated conversations between 'traditionalists' and some of the women bishops at the Lambeth Conference. These informal conversations proved fruitful to the extent that a substantive amendment to a resolution on the Eames Commission was proposed by Bishop Penelope Jamieson of Dunedin (New Zealand), seconded by Bishop Victoria Matthews of Edmonton (Canada), and was spoken to by both Bishop Barnes of Richborough and myself. The amendment – which was passed by a large (70 per cent) majority – affirmed that both those who assent to and those who dissent from the ordination of women to the priesthood and episcopate were loyal Anglicans; that reception was a 'long and spiritual process'; and that no bishop should be forced to ordain or license anyone against his conscience. I was glad to be able to remind the Conference that Anglicans did not believe in making infallible decisions, and that, if they did not believe in making infallible decisions, there was therefore a certain provisionality about the ordination of women to the priesthood, and indeed, the episcopate. There is no doubt that women bishops create even more ecclesiological problems than women priests, and the kind of structured tolerance that the Episcopal Ministry Act of Synod represents in the dioceses of the Church of England would be all but unworkable in a situation in which there were women in the episcopate. That of itself may be a powerful argument for staying our hand at the place at which we have arrived until it becomes a good deal clearer than it is now that a move to consecrate women bishops in the Church of England would be a move that would enhance, and not further undermine, the unity of the Church.

In the end the issues with which we wrestle are issues of

authority, the authority of Scripture, the authority of tradition, the authority of provincial synods in a divided church. And the questions do not go away just because a particular decision has been taken. It was naive optimism to think that simply by passing legislation agreement would be reached, and if there was no agreement then the options were simple – all who disagree must leave (doctrine has been defined), or a way must be sought to accommodate those who stand by the tradition. The Church of England, not surprisingly, chose the second option, and was therefore faced with the challenge, in the words of my title, of learning to live with division: not just a grudging toleration, but a prayerful mutuality of understanding. I think there are signs that the Church of England has been able to move towards that, though it will always be easy to delude ourselves that everyone agrees with our view, or that the 1992 vote has not happened. So the words with which I ended my 1992 Margaret Street sermon still need to be heeded:

> Christians have never been able to expect that their Christian life is free of suffering. We are called rather into a fellowship with Christ in *his* suffering. When we celebrate the Eucharist and receive his life, we are so joined to his sacrifice, that 'we are drawn into the movement of his self-offering'. That is to be the ground of our prayer at all times and in all places, that we may be conformed to the likeness of Christ and come at last to the city of the great King. It may be that our journey in the years immediately ahead may make us more conscious of the pain of division than of unity, for it will be difficult for all to live in a church where there is only a partially accepted ministry in the order of priesthood. But nothing is outside of the love of God; and his Spirit may turn all things to prayer.

This is a revised version of a paper given at a consultation in April 1998 at St George's House, Windsor, offering pastoral reflections on the Episcopal Ministry Act of Synod 1993, and incorporates material delivered as the All Saints' Lecture 1998 at Kellogg College, Oxford.

9

THE EPISCOPAL MINISTRY ACT OF SYNOD 1993
A 'Bearable Anomaly'?

Paul Avis

I begin with a personal statement. I approach the issues raised by the Episcopal Ministry Act of Synod *1993* with mixed feelings. I find my sympathies being pulled in two directions at once. So my views will not be entirely palatable either to those who invoke the provisions of the Act or to those who deplore it as as an 'Act of Folly'.[1] On the one hand, I have been a long-standing advocate of women priests, both in the Diocese of Exeter and in the General Synod, and I have supported the cause through various writings.[2] As an incumbent, I sponsored several women candidates for ordination and played a part in the training of them and others. On the other hand, I believe that the consequences, for the Church of England and for ecumenism, of the General Synod's decision to allow women to become priests are for the time being almost as important as the decision itself.

I have argued consistently that serious theological justification was needed for this step, in terms both of a doctrine of ordained ministry that would support it and of an understanding of authority in a divided Christendom

---

[1] M. Furlong (ed.), *Act of Synod: Act of Folly* (London: SCM Press, 1998).
[2] P. Avis, *Eros and the Sacred* (London: SPCK, 1989), *Anglican Orders and the Priesting of Women* (London: Darton, Longman & Todd for Affirming Catholicism, 1998).

that would justify it. I must confess that I have not always found the theological basis that I was looking for. It seems that the vital issues of catholicity, of scriptural and traditional authority and of holy order – issues that must be addressed in this connection – are typically raised by those from the traditional Anglican constituency. Given our inveterate tendency as Anglicans to benevolent pragmatism, we should privilege those voices that insist on theological and particularly ecclesiological principles being heeded.

I find my indignation aroused in equal measure by, on the one hand, acts of discourtesy and discrimination offered to women priests by those who oppose their priestly ministry and by on the other, any well-founded suspicion that, as a church, we are not keeping faith with those who rely on the Episcopal Ministry Act of Synod *1993* to remain within the Church of England. I will defend those who cannot yet accept this development, because I think that I understand their reasons, even though I do not agree with their conclusions. I am personally committed to the spirit and the letter of the Episcopal Ministry Act of Synod and I believe that it can facilitate a period of open reception, discernment and dialogue.

In the Church of England and in some other churches of the Anglican Communion there is still much heart-searching as to how the majority who accept the ordination of women to the priesthood and the significant minority who remain opposed in conscience might be held together in communion. The fundamental question is how in fact a church that is divided on this issue, to the extent that communion is impaired, can remain one church and how the Anglican Communion can remain truly a communion. Perhaps the issue is felt nowhere more acutely than in the Church of England, which has also gone further than any other Anglican church to accommodate conscientious objectors to the priesting of women. From my position, which aspires to be a mediating one, my central concern can be put quite bluntly: in a commendable attempt to maintain its unity, even in a state of impaired communion, the Church of England has admitted a crucial ambiguity into its ecclesiology. The General Synod, following the lead offered by the House of Bishops, accepted that this ambiguity was the price that had to be paid to secure the priesting of women without producing a schism. This ecclesiological ambiguity focuses on three areas of concern: (1) the unity of the local church (diocese); (2) the unity of the diocesan bishop's ministry; (3) the unity of the *koinonia* of the baptismal/eucharistic community.

The Local Church and the Catholic Church

The first area of concern is the theological understanding – or rather the lack of it – of the local church that is presupposed by the Episcopal Ministry Act of Synod. The Second Vatican Council (1962–5) gave the impetus for the rediscovery of the doctrine of the local church within the Roman Catholic Church. The local church may be defined as the sphere of oversight within which the diocesan bishop exercises his ministry. It is the community of word, sacrament and pastoral responsibility within which the bishop presides. Beyond the local church there is a communion of local churches or dioceses which make up the Catholic Church. Vatican II saw the diocese, under the pastoral rule of the bishop and in communion with him, as the fundamental unit of the Christian Church. On this model, dioceses comprise the operative units of the Church. The diocese is a 'particular' or 'local' church. In other words, it is the *locus* of the Church. It is as much the Church as the whole Catholic Church is the Church. *Lumen gentium* states: 'The individual bishops, who are placed in charge of particular Churches, exercise their pastoral government over the portion of the People of God committed to their care'

(LG 23).[3] This decree on the Church affirms that bishops govern the particular churches entrusted to them as 'vicars and ambassadors of Christ' (LG 27; Abbott, p. 51). And it points out, significantly, that 'every legitimate celebration of the eucharist is regulated by the bishop' (LG 26; Abbott, p. 50).

In the Roman Catholic Church there is debate about the relation between the local church and the universal Church. But what is clear is that, in the teaching of Vatican II, as in the tradition of the Eastern churches, local churches are not catholic because they are fragments of the whole, but they are inherently catholic. There is a universal or catholic Church precisely because there are local churches in communion. The local church is a genuine expression of the Church of Christ that is one, holy, catholic and apostolic. The local church is an instantiation or expression of the one, holy, catholic and apostolic Church. Church unity is manifested in the unity of the local churches within and among themselves. Holiness is nurtured through the means of grace, principally word and sacrament, in liturgical forms, that are entrusted to the whole Church and administered in particular, local communities by those who are authorized to do so. Catholicity is embodied in the communion of local churches which together comprise the universal Church. Apostolicity is transmitted through local churches because apostolic succession is a succession of and within community, embodied in its most representative person, the bishops, and expressed in the visible continuity of episcopal consecrations and of episcopal succession within a see.

The ministry of the bishop, as the focal, representative person of this local Christian community, expresses and embodies the credal marks of the Church: unity, holiness,

---

[3] W.M. Abbott (ed.), *The Documents of Vatican II* (London and Dublin: Geoffrey Chapman, 1966), p. 44. Hereinafter page references to the Abbott edition are given in the main text.

catholicity and apostolicity.[4] It is fundamental to the episcopal polity that Anglicans share with Roman Catholics, Orthodox, Old Catholics and some Lutherans, that the bishop is the chief minister of the local church, the diocese, and its eucharistic president. In the full communion between the bishop and the clergy and laity of the diocese the nature of the Church as one, holy, catholic and apostolic can come to expression.

The decree of Vatican II on bishops *Christus Dominus* reinforces this teaching. A diocese, it states, 'is that portion of God's people which is entrusted to a bishop to be shepherded by him with the cooperation of the presbyters'. It continues: 'Adhering thus to its pastor and gathered together by him in the Holy Spirit through the gospel and the eucharist, this portion constitutes a particular Church in which the one, holy, catholic and apostolic Church of Christ is truly present and operative' (CD 11; Abbott, p. 403).

The decree on the liturgy (*Sacrosanctum concilium*) urges all Christians to hold in high esteem the sacramental life of the diocese centred around the bishop, and it concludes the point in these words: 'Let them be persuaded that the Church reveals herself most clearly when a full complement of God's holy people, united in prayer and a common liturgical service (especially the Eucharist), exercise a thorough and active participation at the very altar where the bishop presides in the company of his priests and other assistants' (SC 41; Abbott, p. 152).

The emphasis of Roman Catholic ecclesiology on the diocese as the local church, the sphere of the bishop's ministry, means that the notion that individual priests and laity can somehow evade or circumvent the sacramental and pastoral ministry of their diocesan bishop ('distance them-

[4] See P. Avis, 'Episcopacy in Relation to the Foundation and Form of the Church', a paper given at the fourth theological conference between the Church of England and the Evangelische Kirche in Deutschland, 2001.

selves' from it, as we sometimes say) would not be an option in the Roman Catholic Church. In the context of Roman Catholic ecclesiology it is inconceivable.

Working within the provisions of the Episcopal Ministry Act of Synod, we could profitably ask whether the unity and integrity of the diocese as the local church could be strengthened. The crucial point here is that the oversight of the diocesan bishop as chief pastor, which is pivotal for the existence of the Church in that place, should not be marginalized or undermined. The appointment of Provincial Episcopal Visitors as Assistant Bishops in a diocese integrates them with the ministry of the diocesan, strengthens the collegiality between all bishops in the diocese and visibly manifests the communion that necessarily obtains between them in the local church.

The Integrity of the Bishop's Ministry

The second area of theological concern has to do with the integrity or unity of the bishop's ministry in the diocese (local church). It is broadly agreed in episcopally ordered churches that the ministry of the bishop is threefold: to teach (through the ministry of the word), to sanctify (through the ministry of the sacraments and liturgy) and to lead or govern (through the ministry of oversight). Vatican II helped to clarify the understanding of episcopal ministry for all churches so ordered. The teaching of Vatican II was innovative in two respects. First, it broadened the traditional Roman Catholic understanding of the bishop's ministry, which had tended to be too heavily focused on the governing authority or jurisdiction of a bishop (a standard view, going back to medieval theology, saw the bishop merely as a priest with enlarged jurisdiction). Second, and more controversially, the Council saw the episcopate as the fullest expression of the sacrament of holy orders and the paradigm of all ministry, from which the priesthood, diaconate and lay ministry are in a sense derived (LG 21; Abbott, p. 41).[5]

The Second Vatican Council's decree on the liturgy *Sacrosanctum concilium* uses language with which many Anglicans would not feel entirely comfortable when it calls the bishop 'the high priest of his flock', and claims that 'in a certain sense it is from him that the faithful who are under his care derive and maintain their life in Christ' (SC 41; Abbott, p. 152). The key issue here is that in Vatican II the ministry of the bishop is seen as actually constitutive of the local church as a church of Christ. These statements are more than a little tinged with the typical Roman Catholic hierarchical conception of authority and sacramental grace, flowing down from above to below, from Christ to the pope, from the pope to the bishops, from the bishops to the priests, from the priests to the laity (in contrast to the approach of the Conciliar tradition which sees the gifts of ministry and authority as given by Christ to the whole body of the Church and then expressed or executed through various instruments or offices). So in quoting these teachings that I can accept only in a qualified sense, I am making an *ad hominem* point about the high doctrine of the episcopate held by the Roman Catholic Church and the seriousness with which it takes the teaching, sanctifying and governing ministry of the diocesan bishop.

The formularies of the Church of England broadly share this theology of the episcopate, though without the hierarchical, pyramidal connotations. The Canons of the Church of England state that 'every bishop is the chief pastor of all that are within his diocese, as well laity as clergy, and their father in God,' and that 'every bishop is, within his diocese,

---

[5] K. Osborne, *Priesthood: A History of the Ordained Ministry in the Roman Catholic Church* (New York: Paulist Press, 1988). A. Barratt, 'The Sacrament of Order and the Second Vatican Council: The Presbyter–Bishop Relationship Revisited', *International Journal for the Study of the Christian Church* 2.2 (2002): 7–27.

the principal minister' (Canon C18). Similarly, the report of the Archbishops' Group on the Episcopate, *Episcopal Ministry*, affirms that the bishop is chief minister in his diocese and the 'eucharistic head of the local diocesan community'. It states that in Anglican polity 'the diocese remains in principle a single eucharistic community'.[6]

Significantly for our discussion, the report insists that the bishop's jurisdiction cannot be detached from his other episcopal roles: 'Oversight and pastoral care can never be separated.'[7] The well-known words of St Ignatius of Antioch from the immediately post-apostolic Church are quoted in the report: 'Be careful, then, to observe a single Eucharist' – for, Ignatius added, there is one flesh, one cup and one bishop. That is to say that unity in the sacraments requires not only the proper use of the elements ordained by Christ, but also unity in the presidency of the Eucharist. Cyprian, from the mid-third century, is also invoked: 'The Church is the people united to its shepherd. From this you should know that the bishop is in the Church and the Church in the bishop.' That is to say that the mutual indwelling of the flock and its Good Shepherd Jesus Christ cannot be assumed without the mutual indwelling of the people of the local church and their chief under-shepherd the bishop. Furthermore, this mutual indwelling is expressed sacramentally. On this point the report concludes that the belief that the bishop is the principal eucharistic president of the local diocesan community belongs to the bedrock understanding of the bishop's role, from the sixteenth century onwards.[8]

There may be a working assumption in some quarters that the Provincial Episcopal Visitor (PEV) or other visiting

---

[6] *Episcopal Ministry* (London: Church House Publishing, 1990), pp. 90, 88 (paras 195, 190).
[7] Ibid., p. 89 (para. 191).
[8] Ibid., p. 27 (paras 62–3).

bishop in effect takes the place of the diocesan. Some might say, 'Yes, we agree with all you have said about the vital, constitutive role of the bishop. His teaching, sanctifying and governing ministry is indeed fundamental – but we apply it to the visiting bishop.' However, there is a subtle but important distinction between 'in place of' and 'on behalf of'. It is acceptable for the PEV to be seen as an extension of the ministry of the diocesan bishop, as his *alter ego*, as any suffragan is. That seems to be what the Episcopal Ministry Act of Synod intends. It would not be ecclesiologically acceptable, in an episcopally ordered church, for the PEV to be regarded as an alternative to the diocesan, to be received 'instead of' him. I therefore question whether Provincial Episcopal *Visitor* is the best term for designating this ministry. The PEV should not be a visitor at all, in the normal sense of the word, but should belong to the diocesan fellowship and family – not a stranger but a member of the household.

There is some talk about a diocese for traditionalists being not territorial but communal and the precedents for 'cultural episcopacy' in the antipodes are sometimes invoked. The Forward in Faith 'Agreed Statement on Communion' goes as far as to suggest that visiting bishops have their own college of priests. Is 'college' here meant metaphorically? If it is meant straightforwardly, in terms of the doctrine of collegiality, it seems highly suspect. Collegiality is primarily between bishops but may be predicated in a secondary sense of the fraternal solidarity between bishops, presbyters and deacons. But in a diocese there can be only one college of presbyters, in communion with the bishop. I cannot see how the idea of a separate college of presbyters, in communion with a PEV, but in a merely impaired state of communion with the diocesan, can avoid being in effect schismatical. It would also raise fundamental questions of oversight (which is safeguarded by the Episcopal Ministry Act of Synod), such as: to whom should the oath of canonical obedience be made?

Talk of communal not territorial dioceses and of alternative colleges is a slippery slope, and I do not think that reflecting Anglican Catholics will want to embark on it. The notion of designated dioceses for special constituencies leads logically to manifold parallel jurisdictions, rampant private judgement as individuals choose their own bishop, and portends a postmodernistic dissolution of community, tradition, authority and order. The notion that a visiting bishop can fulfil some of the proper canonical functions of the diocesan on his behalf is neater and less dangerous. But there are three reasons why a visiting bishop cannot be substituted for the diocesan.

- The first reason why a PEV cannot substitute for the diocesan is that the theological integrity of the diocesan bishop's ministry is inextricably connected with his *locus* in the local church. The bishop *teaches* through the ministry of the word himself and by making provision for and overseeing a ministry of the word in the local church, through ordained ministers, with lay ministers assisting. He *sanctifies* through the ministry of the sacraments and by making provision for and overseeing a sacramental ministry in the local church, through ordained ministers, with lay ministers assisting. He *governs* or leads through the exercise of *episkopē* or pastoral oversight and by making provision for and overseeing the ministry of *episkopē* in the local church through ordained ministers, with lay ministers assisting. As the one who exercises ministry in person and provides ministry by commissioning others to act on his behalf, the bishop of the local church has a unique and irreplaceable ministry to carry forward the mission of the Church through word, sacrament and pastoral oversight.
- The second reason why the PEV cannot substitute for the diocesan is that the ministry of the bishop of the

local church, as the principal teacher of the faith, the principal minister of the sacraments and the chief pastor, is not exercised in isolation but in fellowship, collaboration and collegiality with others. The bishop teaches, sanctifies and governs (or leads) his people in partnership with presbyters, deacons and laity. This partnership or form of collegiality becomes focused and expressed through the conciliar structures of the Church when bishops, clergy and laity sit together as distinct 'houses' in the diocesan synod, each bringing their particular concerns, experiences and insights to bear on issues facing the Church as a whole. It belongs to the diocesan bishop's oversight that he presides at meetings of the diocesan synod. Clergy and laity share this presidency as each of those houses of clergy and laity elect a vice-president. Conciliarity is thus not only an expression of communion but also of shared ministry, of collegiality.

- The third reason why the PEV cannot substitute for the diocesan is that there is a further intimate connection between the ministry of the diocesan bishop and the ministry of priests and deacons in a local church. The clergy of the diocese have been called, tested, trained, ordained, licensed and overseen in their ministry through the instrumentality of the bishop. It is no exaggeration to say that without the bishop's involvement they have no recognized public ministry. They cannot exercise their ministry apart from the bishop's authority. It may be putting the matter too strongly to say that they do so by delegation from the bishop. It sounds better to say that they do so in fellowship, partnership and collegiality with the bishop and under his oversight. But it is certainly true that they do so by authority of the bishop and not without that authority. The cure of souls of the whole diocese, which is entrusted to the bishop, cannot be exercised by him directly and in person, but is shared with the clergy. It is 'both thine and mine'. In this way, the Church today acts in continuity with the Early Church, where the bishop was originally the actual president of the one gathered eucharistic community and personally extended pastoral care to all his people, but involved presbyters in the exercise of that pastoral care. There is, to my mind, a theological impossibility in the notion that a priest can be not in full communion with his bishop and at the same time continue to function both pastorally and liturgically in his parish, for the simple reason that, in an episcopally ordered church, the ministry he is exercising is not his alone but is shared with the bishop, and without the bishop he has no ministry. So it is not only PEVs who exercise an extended form of the bishop's ministry: the presbyters of the diocese – mainly parochial clergy – also do this and should see themselves in this light.

It is becoming clear, as our discussion proceeds, that the unity of the bishop's ministry is not fully safeguarded by the Episcopal Ministry Act of Synod 1993. The Act needs to be interpreted and applied sensitively in order to minimize the damage. The arrangements that the Church of England has approved for conscientious objectors to the ordination of women priests, under this Act of Synod, allows those who oppose the priesting of women to decline the sacramental ministry of their diocesan bishop in the Eucharist, confirmation and ordination. It also has the effect of providing an extended source of pastoral care in fraternal counsel, supervision and guidance. Both pastoral care and sacramental ministry may be provided by Provincial Episcopal Visitors or bishops from a neighbouring diocese or suffragans within the diocese (provincial, regional and diocesan arrangements). The document *Being in Communion* properly insists that 'oversight remains with the diocesan bishop, who remains the focus of unity in his diocese even when he chooses to extend his oversight through another bishop'.[9] However, the Forward in Faith *Agreed Statement on Communion* pushes the boundaries considerably further when it suggests that only legal and financial arrangements remain the concern of the bishop of the diocese – all pastoral matters (including parochial visitations and clergy assessment procedures) becoming the responsibility of the visiting bishop and those he appoints to act for him.

The effect of this interpretation is to reduce pastoral oversight to jurisdiction, to merely legal authority. The diocesan bishop's jurisdiction is protected because any visiting bishops can only operate at the invitation of the diocesan (though the diocesan is obliged, under the Act of Synod, to extend this invitation when petitioned by a Parochial Church Council according to the prescribed form). So the 'bottom line' of episcopal oversight is thought to be safeguarded. But jurisdiction is only one aspect of the ministry of a bishop, and is not necessarily the most important. Legalities and finance, though not to be despised, cannot be allowed to define the ministry of a bishop in the Church of Christ. A bishop's essential episcopal functions, as primary teacher of the faith, principal minister of the sacraments and chief pastor, are undermined by Forward in Faith's radical interpretation of the Act of Synod. That damages the office of bishop and, if applied more widely, would be subversive of the doctrine of the threefold ministry, of holy order, as received in the Anglican tradition. The Act of Synod itself, though not without its ambiguities, is protected from this destructive effect because it sees PEVs as providing 'extended' not 'alternative' episcopal oversight. But those of more extreme views are in danger of sawing off the branch they are sitting on as catholic Christians who give a high place to the

[9] *Being in Communion* GS Misc. 418 (London: General Synod, 1993).

threefold ministry in historical succession – for this 'holy order' is ensured precisely through the sacramental and overseeing aspects of the bishop's total ministry. I fear they do the cause of catholic ecclesiology a disservice by evacuating the ministry of the diocesan bishop (and after all what other sort of bishop is in mind in the catholic theology of holy order?) of much that gives it its theological significance.

Impairment of Communion

I have deliberately avoided using the expression 'out of communion'. The theology of Vatican II, of the ARCIC report *Church as Communion*[10] and of the work of the Eames Commission has taught us to see the *koinonia* of the Church as broader than the communion that is given and expressed in the Eucharist. Communion is grounded in our fundamental unity with Christ through baptism, whereby we are united with him in his death and resurrection, i.e. in the mystery of redemption, and are incorporated into his mystical Body. Vatican II spoke of a 'real though imperfect communion' (UR 2; cf, Abbott, p. 345; 'a certain though imperfect communion') that is brought about through faith and baptism. It further maintained that baptism 'constitutes a sacramental bond of unity linking all who have been reborn by means of it' (UR 22; Abbott, p. 364). This communion is established not only through baptism but through all the life of grace that we enjoy in the Church, especially through prayer, for there is also a real communion in prayer. Roman Catholic and Anglican ecclesiology (but not Eastern Orthodox ecclesiology) recognizes degrees of communion.

The notion of degrees of communion was of course

[10] Anglican–Roman Catholic International Commission, *Church as Communion* (London: Church House Publishing and CTS, 1991). *The Eames Commission: The Official Reports* (Toronto: Anglican Book Centre, 1994).

developed to describe the relationship *between* churches (between the [Roman] Catholic Church and various churches and 'ecclesial communities', as Vatican II characteristically puts it). In its original setting in Vatican II it was not intended to apply to relationships between people, priests and bishops *within* a given church. The extension of this concept, in the form of 'impaired communion', to describe relations within a church, has enabled Anglicans, particularly in the Church of England, to make some theological sense of their predicament following the legislation to allow women to be priested and the ensuing Act of Synod.

The Eames Commission is therefore absolutely right to insist that we should never say we are 'out of communion'. We cannot be out of communion without being outside the Church altogether. It is more accurate and more appropriate to say that we are in a state of impaired communion. But no impairment of communion can be tolerated with equanimity by Christians because it militates against the wholeness and integrity of the body of Christ. There is a dynamic and a momentum in *koinonia* that seeks to overcome that impairment, just as the human body's natural healing properties will work to heal over a wound.

In my study of *koinonia* published several years ago with the title *Christians in Communion*,[11] I argued (not without a dash of rhetoric, I must admit) that *our primary obligation to our fellow Christians is to be in communion with them*. This is the overriding imperative of life in Christ, grounded in our baptismal incorporation into his body. Our communion with our fellow Christians is inextricably integrated with our communion with Christ. I still believe that. I warm very much, therefore, to the conclusion of the Eames Commission that all parties should actively commit

---

[11] P. Avis, *Christians in Communion* (London: Geoffrey Chapman/Mowbray, 1990).

themselves to maintain the highest degree of communion among themselves. It is good to see this taken up in the Forward in Faith *Agreed Statement on Communion.*

Given the provisions of the Episcopal Ministry Act of Synod 1993, the imperative to maintain the highest degree of communion among ourselves must impose requirements on both sides of the argument over women priests. For the majority it must mean scrupulously observing the spirit as well as the letter of the Act of Synod; actively respecting and defending the freedom in conscience of those opposed. As *Being in Communion* says, there should be no marginalization of anyone on the basis of their conscientious opposition towards the ordination of women to the priesthood in the Church of England. For the minority, I suggest it means invoking the provisions of the Act of Synod reluctantly and to a minimal extent, rather than maximizing the possibilities of impairing communion. As *Being in Communion* again puts it, those who cannot accept the ordination of women to the priesthood should not marginalize themselves by withdrawing from the life and government of the Church except in those matters where conscientious convictions are directly at stake.

There are a couple of particular practical issues involved here, which I would like to highlight in conclusion. The first concerns the question of how far the impairment of communion should go.

- I do not believe that those opposed should extend that impairment to members of the presbyteral college who are in communion with a bishop who has ordained women or are in communion with women priests themselves (as proposed in the Forward in Faith *Agreed Statement on Communion*). I have not seen this convincingly justified. It raises suspicions that a 'theology of taint' and of 'guilt by association' is operating here – and that has been disowned repeatedly by opponents of the priesting of women. In order to be consistent on that point, opposers should also completely withdraw from the conciliar structures of the Church at every level, because conciliarity presupposes communion and is a vital expression of it. No-one wants to see 'traditionalists' take that step.

- I do not believe that impairment of communion should extend to a bishop who ordains women. If, as both the House of Bishops and Forward in Faith have stated, that act of ordination does not invalidate the bishop's sacramental ministry as a whole, then priests and parishes should continue to receive that ministry. Talk of 'distancing oneself', employed in the General Synod debate on the Act of Synod, may be true to human nature, but is hardly the language of Zion. This means that I do not think that the central provisions of the Act of Synod are, in strict theology, necessary. I do not think they are required on the basis of theological principles of communion. However, the reality that we are dealing with is that some people, in all conscience, believe that they are necessary. That is the sole reason for the original provisions and for continuing to stand by them.

- However, no-one should have the ministrations forced upon them of a person about whose orders they are doubtful. If they do not believe that a woman priest is truly a priest (in spite of the Church holding that they are duly and canonically ordained) then alternative provision should be made. Resolutions A and B (which, we do well to remember, belong to the original legislation of 1992, not to the Act of Synod 1993) seem to apply to this situation. This approach is different in principle from wishing to 'distance' oneself from someone whom one still regards as a bishop or priest, in spite of deploring particular actions of theirs.

The second practical issue concerns the relation of bishops

ministering under the Episcopal Ministry Act of Synod to the college of bishops. As the teaching of Vatican II suggests, collegiality requires that a bishop becomes a member of the episcopal college not only by consecration, but also by communion with all his fellow bishops (in the Roman Catholic context, by 'hierarchical communion' with the Pope as head of the episcopal college). Membership of the college is dependent on continuing in full communion, and this must, by definition, include eucharistic communion. In Anglicanism this is signified and expressed by being in communion with the metropolitan – for the Church of England this means the Archbishop of Canterbury or the Archbishop of York. PEVs are also, of course, suffragans of the archbishops, which further strengthens their collegiality with them. Communion cannot be impaired to the extent of bishops opposed to the ordination of women priests and operating under the Act of Synod being out of full (i.e. eucharistic) communion with their archbishop, who is also their diocesan, as well as being their metropolitan, and with the college of bishops in communion with him. As the statement of the House of Bishops, following their Manchester meeting in January 1993, put it: 'We envisage that any bishop appointed to assist us in making any extended sacramental provision will remain in full communion with all members of the House of Bishops irrespective of whether or not such members have ordained women priests.' Where there is a diocesan arrangement for the provision of extended episcopal oversight to those who require it (that is to say where a suffragan bishop within the diocese provides this ministry at the direction of the diocesan), this fundamental 'being in communion' is manifest; but the same principle applies across the board – to regional and provincial arrangements too.

Conclusions

In the General Synod, I gave qualified support to the Act of
Synod in my speech and voted for it. I continue to stand by
the Act of Synod – though with a heavy heart and some
misgivings. I am convinced that the Church of England
should keep faith with those who depend on the Act to
remain, in conscience, within her fellowship. I see the Act
continuing to function as long as there is a significant
community of people who invoke it. Many of our problems
are not caused by the Act itself but by a tendency on the
part of some to push matters well beyond its provisions and
to take the impairment of communion to an extreme.
Criticisms of the Act are commonly premised on erroneous
interpretations.

In view of the ecclesiological ambiguities that it involves,
I can only reconcile myself to the Act of Synod as a temporary pastoral accommodation – what the Eames
Commission called 'a strictly extraordinary anomaly in
preference to schism'. The history of the Christian Church is
full of anomalies, but that is no reason to be complacent
about them. While the Act of Synod may be necessary as
the lesser of two evils, the fact remains that it is damaging
to the local church, to the ministry of the bishop and to the
communion that sustains the Church in being. Where the
essential *koinonia* of a church has been damaged, it can never
be too soon for us to try to repair the damage. Within the
constraints of the Act of Synod, we should try to maximize
our communion, and that must entail that the provisions of
the Act are invoked reluctantly and to the minimum extent
that is consistent with it fulfilling its purpose.

INDEX OF NAMES

INDEX OF NAMES